Determining Your Legacy:

The Power of Lasting Impressions

D1362329

By

Larry Zachrich

Determining Your Legacy:

The Power of Lasting Impressions

By Larry Zachrich

www.larryzachrich.com

Power of Impressions Publishing

Acknowledgements

All people we encounter in life's journey influence us, as we each represent the sum total of our individual decisions and the impressions of people around us. I began to thank those who have left a lasting impression on me, but I quickly realized that each person I have encountered during my life has provided a positive impact, a negative lesson, or both. For some, your lasting effect is the humility and generosity with which you have handled success. In many cases, your inspiration is the grace and fortitude exhibited during times of adversity. Each of you has provided examples which reinforce the theme of life's lasting impressions.

My parents, James and Delores Zachrich, have certainly left a positive impression on me. I am grateful to Father Stanbery and Father Cunningham for continuous inspirations, and for the influence of Father George, Father Louis, and the Fathers of Mercy, who have certainly improved my chances of being counted among the sheep instead of the goats on the right side of eternity (from Matthew 25: 31 – 46).[1] Time will tell whether they have truly helped to save my soul. I am confident they have served as a motivation and a moral compass for many others. Additionally, I thank Pastor Marcis for many insightful discussions.

I am grateful to those willing to allow their stories to be told and to those whose critique enhanced the quality of writing. Shari Beck, Kirk Fruth, Wally Snyder, Linda Walker, Lynnette Yerbury (Lushena), Charlie Beem, Garry Grau, Father Louis, Monsignor Kubacki, Pastor Marcis, and Annette Craven all took the time to recommend improvements. Your comments inspired the finished product of "Determining Your Legacy".

---

[1] United States Conference of Catholic Bishops, *The New American Bible* (Washington: United States Conference of Catholic Bishops, 2002), 1054.

Contents

Preface

This book is written to illuminate the impact of impressions on our lives and to enhance our ability to perceive those influences. My hope is to promote the importance of lasting impressions and to inspire readers to reflect on the lasting impressions they create. There are three main goals of this book:

1. To be entertaining
2. To be educational
3. To be inspirational

The plan of the book is to recognize the significance of first impressions, but then to identify how first impressions pale in comparison with the long-term influence of lasting impressions. Finally, the importance of lasting impressions leads to conscious effort to determine a legacy, your gift of guidance for others.

The following topics are emphasized:

1. Learning of impressions – who, what, when, where, why, how
2. Understanding impression traits – speed, accuracy, longevity
3. Experiencing examples of impressions – positive and negative
4. Betrayal of impressions – deceit and the consequences
5. Genuine impressions – valuing the importance of perceptions
6. Lessons of lasting impressions – legacies for others to follow
7. Determining lasting impressions – planning a legacy

You will find the significance of first impressions is examined, along with a review of research regarding the speed, accuracy, longevity, and power of first impressions. However, the ability to manipulate impressions is investigated, as deceptive forces can distort first impressions. Additionally, typical errors in perception are examined, as they sometimes betray our ability to develop accurate impressions of others.

My friend, Charlie Beem, clarified lasting impressions for me when he advised, "It is beneficial for us to be reminded of the people in our lives, as none of us completes the journey through life alone." The various impacts people have provided in my life are shared in humorous and enlightening stories alternated within the lessons provided by a study of impressions. You will relive moments in your own life as you reflect on the impact of friends, neighbors, coworkers, and family. The development of a personal lasting impression is then encouraged through specific recommendations for the reader to determine an inspiration, a lasting impression as your legacy for others.

First impression emphasis is a focus on the immediate effect, a short-term memory of sorts, characterized by an inward focus on the self. It is a philosophy of "living in the moment." People with a disposable attitude toward life tend to use other people for their selfish purposes and then quickly discard them. They jump from job to job for short-term gains and ignore the consequences of their actions on others. The attitudes of those who overemphasize first impressions center on "What's in it for me?", "What have you done for me lately?", and "How can I gain in the short term no matter the long term cost?"

A lasting impression emphasis is a focus on the lasting impact, a long-term memory in a way, which is characterized by an outward focus on others. It is a philosophy of "planning for the future." People with a genuine life-long focus cultivate friendships with others, value long-term relationships, and maintain long career employment stability. The thinking of those who value lasting impressions is "How can I help others?", "What are the needs of others?", and "How can I best advance the long-term benefit of all?"

While a first impression is often fast, accurate, and long-lasting, it is only an initial reaction to a stranger. In most cases there will be later encounters which provide additional information over a broader range of experiences and a longer time frame. When there are opportunities to interact over many years and in a variety of circumstances, the observer will learn to modify the first perception and validate an accurate impression.

For most people a long-term relationship develops a genuine impression which is cemented for life. When a connection with someone is later ended through death, retirement, relocation, or another event, the final impact of that person becomes their lasting impression. When we become aware of our influence on others around us, we may think more carefully about our actions and consider our impact on others. As we steer the development of our lasting impression, we create our legacy, which is also our contribution to those who follow us.

"Determining Your Legacy" was written to illuminate the impact of impressions on our lives and to enhance our ability to perceive those influences. The power of impressions is revealed through real-life stories, and the significance of lasting impressions on life's decisions is clarified. Once we realize the power of genuine impressions, we may determine our lasting legacy for others as a contribution to those who follow us.

Chapter 1
Impression Awareness

"The characteristic of a great man is his power to leave a lasting impression on people he meets."[1] – Winston Churchill

"Help us, Frank! What should we do?" a coworker screamed.

Frank's shoulder had slammed into the doorway. He steadied himself with both hands on the wall as he stared toward the ceiling. The explosion somewhere above the fluorescent lights was nearly enough to knock a full-grown man off his feet. Frank felt the entire building sway off center, then slowly return to its original position. Men and women ran out of offices into the lobby area with puzzled expressions. This had never happened in their office building, but they all knew Frank was a construction manager. His calm leadership was predictable and the others knew they could count on his decisions.

Before Frank could respond, a dazed woman in a charred dress staggered toward them from the hallway where the bang seemed to originate. Her glazed eyes stared straight ahead and her mouth was half open, a trickle of blood oozing down from her scalp across a soot-covered cheek. Behind her the floor smoldered where the carpet met black holes in the wall, empty shafts where elevators had once carried employees downward at the end of each shift. Smoke billowed from the adjacent stairwell where emergency lights were flickering and the door was tilted open, torn loose from two of its three hinges.

"Take her by the arms!" Frank exclaimed, as he glanced past the woman toward the open elevator doors. A man on each side grabbed her by the wrists just as the woman's knees started to buckle. "Get a seat for her," Frank shouted, and someone slid a

1

chair on wheels into the hallway. Once the woman was seated, Frank told a man to bring a cup of water and some towels from the restroom. Coworkers wiped soot off the lady's face and checked the blackened dress to see if she had suffered burns to her skin. As they assisted the woman, Frank rushed past them into the hallway.

Shattered ceiling panels littered the floor and flames erupted from the top of the wall where elevators previously stood. Frank and Nicole locked eyes for a moment, as Frank shook his head and shrugged his shoulders. They were both stunned. Just a moment earlier, Nicole and Frank De Martini had been casually sipping coffee with a picturesque view of the late summer sky in a perfect shade of deep blue. Outside the office window an orange sunrise reflected off the many tall buildings. Unlike most couples, they worked on the same block and had carpooled together into the city to enjoy each other's company as their typical morning routine. Today they were chatting in Frank's office until it was time for Nicole to descend to street level and complete the ten-minute walk to her cubicle in the adjacent building. From her seat near the window, Nicole had been watching the tiny cars 88 floors below as drivers began the day, much like any other. However, this morning was anything but normal.

Frank grabbed the radio at his waist where the strap cradled it each day as a manager with the Port Authority. In a professional tone of voice, he reported fire and smoke to the dispatcher, who replied to verify that the emergency was on the 88th floor. Frank was quickly joined by a coworker, Construction Inspector Pablo Ortiz, who had already searched for an escape route. He reported, "Stairway C is our best choice. But we have to climb over a pile of debris and ceiling panels that have dropped onto the floor."[2]

Frank and Pablo directed people toward the only available stairs. Frank assured Nicole that she should leave and that he would follow closely behind her. He and Pablo then combed every office on the 88th floor to clear out any stragglers. Before heading for the stairwell, Frank grabbed two hard hats, a second radio, and a flashlight from the building inspection office, while Pablo emerged from his cubicle with a crowbar. "As they stepped into the stairway, they could hear pounding from above."[3] After one glance at each other, Frank and Pablo raced upward.

They found the stairwell door jammed at the 89th floor where people were banging and yelling. Many had desperately thrown themselves into the door several times, but to no avail. Searing flames and black smoke pouring from the north side of the building had chased them toward Stairway C as their only hope. They were already breathing through wet towels as smoke engulfed the hallway. Most of the workers on level 89 had already phoned family members for what they assumed was their final conversation. Some were holed up in their offices as a last stand with a jacket or sweater stuffed into the gap at the bottom of their door to block the smoke.

Those still hitting the stairway door in vain were surprised by a crowbar smashing through the drywall beside the doorway. Pablo was tearing through the wall between metal studs to cut open enough space for people to escape. Once Pablo and Frank had climbed through the gap beside the door, the others crawled out of the hole and into the stairway. The two quickly inspected each office to make certain the floor was clear of workers. The last resident to leave the 89th floor expected that Frank and Pablo would descend closely behind, but he caught a glimpse of them turning up the stairs instead.

On the 90th floor, smoke billowed through the hallways as people milled about, uncertain what to do without functioning elevators and finding two of the stairways blocked. A moving white light flashed through the haze from one office to another as the two rescuers quickly pointed people toward the useable stairway. Once they knew the path to a safe exit, there was no stopping the stream of survivors as they joined the exodus. The 90th floor was soon deserted just as quickly as the last two levels had been vacated.

Employees on the 86th and 87th floors also recalled seeing two men in hardhats emerge through the smoke to lead them out. Their story was similar to that of others, as they were led to Stairway C by two good Samaritans whom they assumed were directed to them after their frantic calls to the switchboard. However, they later learned that their rescuers had voluntarily sought out people in need. Only afterward was the extent of their rescue effort truly appreciated. Frank and Pablo had cleared each floor down to level 78, where they were last seen trying to free a coworker from an elevator in the north tower of the World Trade Center on September 11. Their lasting impression is one of unselfish heroics which directly saved seventy-seven people from the collapse of the tower, but the two of them did not get out in time.[4]

Journey to Honor a Friend

"I still can't get over that Frank De Martini and his friend," Pete exclaimed to his wife as he stared out the passenger window of their moving car. "It's hard to believe that fifteen years have passed since the twin towers collapsed, but we watched their story retold just last night on television."

"Those two saved a lot of lives," Julie replied, glancing into the rearview mirror.

"I guess bravery is contagious when you're in the moment because they both jumped into action," Pete responded. "At least they had each other to lean on in their final minutes."

Julie answered, "Their story has left an amazing impression on people. It's actually a lot like the impact of characters in the book that Larry wrote and their effect on others."

4

"His book is the reason for this trip, after all," Pete commented. "We won't forget this impression right away either."

Their car sped past rolling hills and ripe, tall cornfields with the driver focused intently on the road ahead as the lone passenger held a wrinkled map close to his face, squinting at the colored lines. He adjusted the pages once again, refolding and turning them from side to side as if a different angle would reveal the information which had thus far eluded him. He eventually lowered the map and turned to the driver.

"I still can't determine which direction rivers flow in this area," Pete declared. "The water either drains north toward the Ohio River or travels west to the Mississippi, but I can't tell where the watershed changes on this map."

"Your map isn't better than the Garmin after all," his wife, Julie, replied with a smile as she steered the car past slower traffic.

"You know I gain much more satisfaction from reading maps than I would ever get from that Garmin woman!" Pete retorted, verbalizing his disdain for GPS technology. "I would hate to see you put too much confidence in her. She's not that impressive."

"Well, I'd say she's doing alright. She's gotten us this far," Julie commented with outstretched arm, her open palm waving slowly left to right as she relied upon the landscape as evidence.

"Don't give that Garmin more credit than she deserves," Pete responded, "We've made it this far because Alice sent us good directions. Besides, we are really just following the other two cars. My impression of the Garmin woman is that she is overrated."

Temporarily overlooking her husband's reply, Julie searched both sides of the highway for a landmark. "We must have traveled almost nine miles by now," stated Julie, as she glanced at the odometer. "It should be time for the next step of the directions. What is our next turn according to the paper Alice gave us?"

"Why don't you just ask the Garmin if you think she's so smart?" Pete wondered to himself, but then thought of a more diplomatic reply.

"The directions tell us to turn left after nine miles onto Shakertown Road. Then we turn right on Shaker Museum Road and drive for just a short distance," Pete responded. "We should be getting very close to the Chapel. By the way, do you have any idea who the Shakers were?" he asked her.

"No, but I am sure my history husband will tell me," Julie answered as she pressed the lever to activate the turn signal. She steered the car into a left turn, following the other two vehicles which had already rounded the corner.

"They were an offshoot of the Quakers and they also tended to live in colonies," Pete explained, "and you'd better be a hard worker if you wanted to be a Shaker. They were serious all of the time and for them life was about being useful. In some of their colonies the men and women lived in separate buildings."

"There are times I'd find that beneficial," Julie replied with a chuckle. "Those Shakers might have been onto something!"

"You should know by now that too many women together in one place is just a room full of trouble," Pete retorted, then smiled to himself. "I wouldn't want to be in the middle of that, but it might be entertaining to watch."

Julie shook her head and decided to ignore him. After a right turn, she stated, "The other cars are slowing. I think we have arrived at the Chapel."

The conversation in the lead car had focused on baseball and the impact of heroes and villains on the sport. "A dishonest ballplayer like Mark McGwire is way different from a hero like Cal Ripken, Jr.," Kirk stated. "One would rather inject drugs to help him hit home runs, while the other worked hard each off-season to stay in shape over many years."

6

Dan replied, "The legacy of one is pretty much a cheater and that's why most sports writers think McGwire has no business being voted into the Baseball Hall of Fame."[5]

Kirk agreed, "You're right. While one is a sports legend with such a positive impression on young players, the other has created a negative perception."

Sandy stated, "In a way, that McGwire makes all players look bad. People will wonder who else is cheating!"

Dan stated, "I guess experience teaches the difference between selfish first impressions and life's worthwhile impressions. Unfortunately, people are drawn to quick first impressions rather than long-term genuine impressions which take more time to appreciate their importance."

Riders in the middle car had been discussing selfish interests in a different way. "Did you hear about that Salvation Army bell ringer that was robbed last Christmas?" Louie asked. "One guy distracted the volunteer, while his accomplice grabbed the kettle. By the time shoppers realized something was wrong, the two had escaped and ruined the Christmas spirit."

"People are often so focused on themselves that they don't comprehend their impression on others, or they just do not care," Wally replied. "I guess there will always be selfish people. They are driven by personal wants instead of true needs, placing themselves ahead of others."[6]

"But some people truly are caring," Darlene stated. "Sam Walton built a retail empire and he really did help people."

Vanessa responded, "It was his wife, Helen, who led the charity. She had a quote, 'It's not what you gather, but what you scatter that tells what kind of life you have lived.'[7] Their foundation has given billions of dollars to charities."[8]

Wally summarized the discussion, "Most people don't recognize they create an impression. If we realize our influence,

7

we might think more carefully about our impact on others. After all, each of us is remembered long after we have left this life."

In the last car, Pete's focus had returned to the anniversary broadcast of the World Trade Center heroes. He stated, "That Frank De Martini and his friend, Pablo, never knew what caused the calamity on September 11, nor were they aware of an imminent collapse of the north tower. They only knew that people needed help. Dozens of survivors and their families will remember that fateful day with gratitude, as they reflect on the memory of the two heroes of the World Trade Center whose unselfish bravery formed a long-term impression. I guess each of us imprints a long-term influence on others, either our last impact or the most compelling one, which is later recalled as our lasting impression."

Arrival at the Chapel

The first car hesitated momentarily at the entrance of the parking lot, and then led all three vehicles forward. They traveled as a caravan that had driven together so the riders would avoid losing their way on the long drive to a destination where none of them had ever traveled.

"Dan, did Larry give you a copy of his book to read?" Kirk asked, as he slowed the first car in the center of the parking lot.

"Yes, I received an autographed copy at Christmas with a personalized note inside the cover," he replied. "I had never read a book by an author I knew."

"It was funny at first, but Larry's book later had a serious impact on me," Kirk explained.

"Where do you think we should park?" Lynette asked, searching the directions in her hand, hoping the paper would reveal the answer to her question.

"Look, someone at the far end of the lot is waving for us," Dan responded as he pointed.

Kirk nudged the car forward, driving past empty parking spaces toward the figure in the distance. He added to his earlier comment, "I actually read the final copy twice. There were some quotes I went back to locate so I could record them."

Squirrels scurried away from the oncoming cars, running into the grass and climbing up the tall oak trees. When each of the vehicles had parked between bright white lines of the newly sealed asphalt, the car doors opened simultaneously.

Women stepped out of the cars and rearranged their dresses, while the men took a moment to pull on suit coats. Straightening their finest apparel, they momentarily waited for all to gather before walking purposefully across the pavement.

"We must have driven most of the way through Kentucky," Julie commented as they turned to stroll up the concrete walkway at the end of the parking lot. Well-groomed shrubs and manicured lawns lined their path as the sidewalk rose slightly up the mild incline toward the church. A gentle breeze started tassels swaying in a nearby sea of cornfields which seemed to extend all the way to the horizon, interrupted periodically by tracts of hardwood trees.

"I'd say we're less than an hour from Nashville," Pete replied.

"You are so right!" commented Wally, who walked up from a different car, but overheard Pete's remark. "The last exit was number 20 and we drove several miles south of that point."

As the friends strolled nearer to the Chapel, high walls of scarlet and tan brick with a red tile roof, the clouds above parted and rays of sunshine poured their warmth from a deep blue sky. Birds chirped loudly, welcoming all to the serene setting in rural southwestern Kentucky. The walkway opened into a large brick patio in front of the Chapel, which evoked ties to St. Peter's square at the Vatican in Rome. A statue of Our Lady of Consolation in the center of the piazza seemed to welcome the group with her calm eyes as they stopped to appreciate the peaceful scene.

9

Hesitating, as those unfamiliar with the location, the party of travelers looked left and right, finally ascending the few steps toward the middle doors. The round limestone arches, representative of the Romanesque style of architecture, highlighted huge bronze doors. As Wally strained to pull open the stubborn metal door, a sliver of light illuminated the threshold, temporarily casting a beam of sunlight into the doorway. Once each of the other travelers had cautiously stepped inside, Wally slipped through the opening and released the heavy door, which creaked loudly and then slammed shut with a metallic thud, throwing the vestibule into total darkness.

Impressions often create a significant impact!

---

[1] Dominique Enright, *The Wicked Wit of Winston Churchill* (London: Michael O'Mara Books Limited, 2001), 10.

[2] Jim Dwyer and Kevin Flynn, *102 Minutes: The Unforgettable Story of the Fight to Survive Inside the Twin Towers* (New York, NY: Times Books, Henry Holt and Company, 2005), 84.

[3] Ibid, p. 85.

[4] "9/11: The Twin Towers," *102 Minutes: The Untold Story of the Fight to Survive Inside the Twin Towers,* Narrated by Harry Pritchett and written by Jim Dwyer and Kevin Flynn, Discovery Channel, aired September 3, 2006, Television.

[5] Zachary D. Rymer, "Why Mark McGwire Doesn't Deserve to Be in Cooperstown*,"* Bleacher Report, last modified December 6, 2012, http://bleacherreport.com/articles/1434532-hall-of-fame-vote-2013-why-mark-mcgwire-doesnt-deserve-to-be-in-cooperstown.

[6] Rev. Msgr. Christopher P. Vasko, *The Twenty-Third Psalm: A Reflection on the Passion of Jesus Christ* (Swanton, OH: Author, 2013), 26.

[7] No Author, "Our Legacy; Our Story – The Walton Family Foundation," accessed September 6, 2013,http://www.waltonfamilyfoundation.org/about.

[8] No Author, "The Walton Family Foundation," accessed September 6, 2013, http://www.waltonfamilyfoundation.org/grantees.

Chapter 2
First Impressions

"First impressions are crucial because they set the stage for future conversations, relationships, and businesses."[1] – Susan Fee

The visitors were momentarily blinded by the shock of leaving the brilliant sunshine, as a few seconds were required for their eyes to adjust to the dim indoor lighting. The group then spotted a familiar face and quickly walked toward her at the entrance of the Chapel and exchanged hugs with my wife, Alice. She was visibly pleased by their arrival, embracing each of them in turn.

"Thank you very much for making the long trip from northwest Ohio," Alice told them.

"We had to come for Larry," Kirk replied.

To make certain they all felt welcome, she introduced them to each other one at a time. "This is Kirk and Lynette, Louie and Vanessa, and Wally and Darlene from Holgate, while Dan and Sandy live near New Bavaria," she explained to Pete and Julie. "Do you know Pete and Julie?" Alice asked the others. "They live between Holgate and New Bavaria."

"You have the orchard on the ridge," Kirk stated.

"Yes, my brothers and I grow apples and press cider," Pete answered. "The business has been in my family for generations."

"We already know you since you also attend Sacred Heart Church," Dan commented.

"Of course," Julie responded. "We see you often."

"Wally, did you own the funeral home in town?" Pete asked.

"That's right," Wally replied. "We managed the funeral home in Holgate and most of us were in Larry and Alice's wedding."

"Kirk and I were in the same class with Larry all the way through school," Louie stated. "In fact, we are about to celebrate our forty-fifth class reunion next summer."

Flashback – Forming Impressions

Forty-five years since I graduated from high school! Our first impressions on each other in grade school had begun a lifetime friendship. I recently realized my friends are still very loyal, as they have not told me I am nuts for writing a book.

"So once again, what is the book you are writing?" my life-long friend, Kirk, had asked me several years earlier.

"I call it 'Determining Your Legacy: The Power of Lasting Impressions'," I replied.

"You'll have to explain what that means," he answered.

"I get that reaction a lot," I had told Kirk. "You are actually in my book. Real-life stories help develop an appreciation for impressions and you are in many of my lasting impression stories, a connection which began more than fifty years ago."

Within a few chapters, the book I handed to him revealed the importance of impressions, including the speed, accuracy, and longevity of impressions. Perceptions lead to conclusions whether the impressions we form are positive or negative. However, the value of impressions immediately dissipates when deception is involved, as false impressions are useless. Genuine impressions then, those developed over the long term, are life's lessons which are treasured for their valuable influence. Once we appreciate the importance of lasting impressions, we may recognize the opportunity to create our own legacy which benefits others. Whether focused on family, professional, or spiritual impacts, our lasting impressions may influence relatives, friends, colleagues, or even strangers, whose lives are enriched by our examples.

Early Impressions

As I reflected on a 57-year friendship with Kirk, I recalled nervously entering the doorway at Holgate Elementary on the first day of school one year. The hallway was long and wide, with nobody in sight as I slowly walked past classrooms of my earlier grades. I didn't know which students from last year would join me and I wasn't even sure which room to enter. I stopped several times to glance at a sign posted outside of each doorway. Finally, the "Grade 4" sign next to an open door listed my name alphabetically at the bottom of the page. Finding the Z for Zachrich, I knew I was in the right place.

I bashfully tiptoed through the doorway of the fourth grade classroom, then saw the profile of my new teacher sitting at her desk with total focus on the pages of the book in her hands. She wore blonde hair wrapped tightly into a bun on the top of her head with a large metal barrette holding it in place. As she sensed my presence, her head slowly turned my direction and she lowered her chin, raising her eyebrows for maximum clarity as she stared at me over her reading glasses. I froze in her gaze, which seemed to last forever as her eyes examined me up and down, assessing my potential as a new recruit. Finally Miss Meyer commented, "Well, that's a pretty blue shirt you're wearing today."

I quickly replied, "Yes, and it matches your eyes."

Her face brightened as she turned her chair toward me, her eyebrows lowered, and she immediately smiled, noticeably impressed with my response. We hit it off at once and initiated a friendship which lasted for many years thereafter. However, in retrospect, I don't think Miss Meyer understood the true meaning of my reply. You see, I didn't have a clue about the color of her eyes, but I don't think I ever saw Miss Meyer without thick makeup painted on the eyelids above her eyes and it was always the brightest shade of blue. Impressions can be unintentional. I had unknowingly established a positive first impression which built a solid foundation for the new school year, starting my journey through fourth grade on the right foot.

Quick First Impressions

"Literally every interaction we have with a new person entails a first impression."[2] The same is true of events we experience for the first time. Our initial reaction is to label the new encounter, and then file it away in memory.

That first impression has been described as a frozen moment, much like an instant Polaroid picture, that develops quickly and never entirely fades. "Often, that snapshot captures important elements of the truth."[3] Like a photograph, the first impression is developed very quickly. As a vivid picture, it immediately triggers our reaction.

The Speed of Chocolate

When I was ten years old, my family vacationed with short camping trips as our funds allowed. One vacation stands out above all others, and that is our family trip to Wisconsin Dells. There are two things I remember about visiting the Dells. First, there was a German Shepherd dog that jumped high in the air from one rock outcrop to another. Secondly, they had a broken candy bar machine. The trained dog show was okay, but the candy machine was incredible.

In those days vending machines were not electronic, but operated with mechanical components. A person would drop a coin into the slot and then pull a knob to release the item. Most kids had a habit, I guess much like checking the coin return on a pay telephone, of testing vending machines. Children would reach out and pull a knob while walking past a machine just in case someone had inadvertently left it ready to dispense an item.

Well, as I followed my parents down the sidewalk near vending machines at Wisconsin Dells, I reached out and grabbed a knob. When I pulled on the handle, a chocolate bar dropped into the tray. I stopped in my tracks, wondering if I could make it happen again. A second pull resulted in another candy bar falling to me. In no time at all, I was yanking knobs with both hands as fast as I could grab them and candy bars were flying everywhere. As soon as my parents saw what was happening, they rushed back to pry my hands off the knobs and my dad scooped me up to haul me away from the candy. I remember my father carrying me in one direction while I screamed with arms outstretched toward the machine, "No, no, those are my candy bars!" The impression of that event was immediate, hitting me as fast as the chocolate bars dropping into the metal tray of the vending machine.

Accurate Impressions

If you think about the last time you tried a new product, you will recall the speed of your perception, probably an immediate impression on you. The opinion was quickly formed and fixed in memory like the impact of a bad restaurant. We seldom consider the sparse nature of information which leads to the formation of impressions, or why we quickly apply them to our decision making process.

In a subconscious way, we allow ourselves to rely upon first impressions because our history of snap judgments has been so accurate in steering past decisions. "And the truth is that our unconscious is really good at this."[4] Accuracy is possible in brief encounters.

An Evil Premonition Turns Out to Be Accurate

When I was 11 years old, a bully lived one block away. He was only a couple of years older, but much bigger than children my age. He seemed like a nasty troll in a scary fairy tale. I had to pass his house on the walk to school and back, to visit my friend, and to make the trip downtown. I would cringe each time I walked past his corner, wondering if that was the day he would jump out at me. When he was waiting there, he might take away my lunch, call me names, or at least force me off the sidewalk, especially on rainy days with large mud puddles.

On one occasion a friend and I were walking my dog, when the bully jumped out at us. My dog immediately barked at him and he picked up the dog and threw it, breaking my dog's leg. I can still recall that my parents had a cast put on the broken leg. The bottom of the metal splint in the cast would "tap, tap, tap" on the linoleum floor in our house. I guess the experience created a memory of early days, my first dog, and growing up in a neighborhood with a bully.

That was also my first impression of true evil. I learned later in life that Steve had become an adult troublemaker, had several brushes with the law, and was later sent to prison. His behavior as a youth led to my negative assessment, which was justified, as pet abuse has proven to be a predictor of domestic violence.[5] The negative impression formed in early years was accurate, as it foretold the painful result of his misguided behavior later in life.

Positive Impressions

Those with pleasant personalities convey a positive image with ease and the favorable view is quickly accepted by observers who believe they can distinguish a genuine favorable impression from a performance which is staged. Most of us strive to create a positive impression as a lasting effect on others because we know favorable perceptions are more successful than negative assessments. Therefore, we employ a great deal of effort to determine a positive impression.

However, genuine positive impressions are usually formed without effort on the part of the subject or the perceiver. The honestly favorable impact is quickly recognized for its value and the one who transmits it is then revered for sharing a positive impression.

Positive Lessons of Work

My father didn't take me to the woodshed for a spanking; he took me there to learn business. A neighbor had given my dad a small building and it was delivered behind a tractor and chain. Once it was dragged onto our country property, my father filled the building with posts, boards, and plywood that we had collected, so we referred to it as "the woodshed."

We attached a wire fence to the shed and bought some chicks, which I fed and watered. My dad taught me how to account for expenses in a notebook and a few months later I recorded the revenue from selling chickens to the butcher. The posts, boards, and plywood came in handy as we reinforced the building and converted it into a hog pen. I recorded expenses and revenue when selling the piglets from several litters over the years. During that experience, my father and I discussed the price of feed, the market for pigs, and profit which was earned. We increased or decreased the number of animals based on the trends in the meat market and grain prices.

Negative Impressions

There are occasions in life when each of us has made a mistake that certainly created a negative impression. I suppose we have all wished we had an opportunity to replay an event. As I have witnessed the effect among people and businesses, the best course of action is to quickly apologize for an offense and to remedy whatever has disappointed others.

It may have been a misspoken word or an inadvertent action. Perhaps we offended someone or maybe a defective product was sold. A negative perception won't disappear immediately, but we can only hope that a positive response and long-term commitment will turn around the negative impression among friends as well as customers.

Not Good Boy Scouts

As a member of the local Boy Scout troop, I attended the Klondike Derby one year along with a couple of dozen other scouts. I still recall it was one of the coldest experiences of my life, as our troop camped outdoors on a snowy weekend in February with few provisions. We fashioned a couple of discarded Christmas trees and a sheet of plastic into a makeshift shelter.

During the daytime there were dogsled races and a variety of contests in which teams competed for the highest score. One of the events required us to start a fire by using flint and steel, usually a long and arduous task. We were expected to create a spark to cause the kindling to smolder, ignite the chips, and eventually build sticks into a fire which would burn through a string that had been drawn across the fire pit at a height of two feet. As it was a timed event, the stopwatch began ticking as soon as a team arrived.

When our group slid to a stop at the fire starting competition, we all jumped into action. One boy removed the kindling from his backpack, another produced the wood chips, a third provided sticks, and two of us positioned ourselves on each side of the pit to fan the smoldering pile. However, it seemed that the third time the steel was clicked, a spark ignited the wood chips and shot a ball of flame into the air, searing through the string. While we cheered and clapped, one of the judges sniffed the remaining wood chips.

"Why do I smell gasoline?" he asked. Sure enough, the kid who brought the wood chips had thought we needed a head start.

That disgraceful impression followed our troop for several years, even if it did seem funny at the time.

Impressions Frozen in Time

You might recall people and situations in your own life which imprinted an immediate impression on you. The image is then committed to memory, from which it is easily recalled when making decisions. At the time events impress us, we seldom realize they will become long-term memories, or even why they stick with us, until a spontaneous moment later in life when those impressions jump to the front of our minds and vividly steer our decisions.

Because our reactions are so fast and typically so accurate, we latch onto impressions and cling to them without much regard for opinions which are contrary. Only after long-held beliefs have persisted, possibly some which were erroneous, do we reconsider our impressions.

Long-Term Impressions

I still remember that in junior high school the right first impression is critical when meeting new friends and establishing popularity. If you're not athletic or attractive at that age, your social status is truly in jeopardy. One clothing mishap, a misspoken word, or the wrong behavioral quirk can be devastating and kids are sometimes unforgiving. For one classmate named Tom, the mistake was his pants pulled a little too far above his waist, which meant they also rode high above his shoes. They were declared "high water pants" by other kids, who often reminded him through their teasing that the first impression they perceived was a wardrobe error.

In ninth grade health class, poor Gerard blurted the wrong answer out loud, which became an instant memory. That day began innocently enough, much like any other school day. Our classroom windows were decorated for the fall season with a variety of leaves cut from brightly colored construction paper and there were black silhouettes of Thanksgiving pilgrims on the wall. Posters of Hubert Humphrey and Richard Nixon headlined the bulletin board, reminders of recent government lessons, as we had followed the presidential election campaign that year. There were diagrams of a male body and a female character, each hanging from a tack in the cork insert at the top of the chalkboard to serve as visual models of body parts for our study of human anatomy in health class.

During a discussion on sexually transmitted diseases, our teacher, Mr. Lockwood, asked, "Does anyone know what the initials VD stand for?"

"Ask Rick," blurted one student, "he should know."

"Yeah, ask the voice of experience!" shouted another boy.

"You guys are just jealous of my good looks", Rick replied. "Don't you wish you were as cool as me?"

The room filled with snickers, as the whole discussion had drawn giggles from the onset and the personal reference to Rick, although not deserved, made it all the funnier. However, the teacher was quickly losing his sense of humor. "Listen up now," he exclaimed in a louder voice. "Who's going to tell me what VD stands for?"

Gerard's hand shot into the air as he anxiously whispered, "I know, I know." Mr. Lockwood's chin dropped. He was as surprised as anyone, since Gerard never responded in class. Other kids, especially the "A" students, were puzzled that he might have the answer. The teacher thought to himself, "Maybe this is Gerard's chance to answer a question!"

"Okay, Gerard," the teacher instructed, "tell us what the letters VD stand for."

Gerard proudly took a deep breath and loudly announced, "Veteran's Day!"

A moment of stunned silence was immediately followed by an explosion of laughter. Even Mr. Lockwood had trouble containing himself in front of the class. Unfortunately, that moment had determined a permanent impression for a hapless student whose ego was crushed. It was a cruel lesson of life and I don't recall that Gerard ever answered out loud again.

The embarrassment reminded me of one of my own errors which was actually beyond my control. Our Boy Scout troop had decided to hike the Heritage Trail, a grueling twenty-one mile trek along the Blanchard River. After an entire day of walking through brush, climbing up and down the river bank, and enduring a hot, crowded car for an hour's ride home, I was dropped off at my grandparents' front yard, where I promptly puked in the grass before the carload of my friends could drive out of sight. It took a while to overcome the stigma of that event, an impression I had not planned.

Overall, I fared well enough at first impressions with classmates and I think all of the kids my age were friends of mine. While many children related to only a small circle of students, I recall having a positive connection with the boys and the girls, among Catholics and Protestants, with town kids and country bus riders, with some who were smarter and others less gifted, and with those who were popular along with the less well liked.

It was especially fun to hang out with the ornery students once in a while. They were much more entertaining than the well behaved kids and they picked on you less often if you seemed to be one of them. I guess I was blessed to figure out that I could be friendly to all and, at least occasionally, to say something funny. Part of growing up is learning what is successful and what doesn't work in order to make a favorable impression on others.

Creating the right first impression is particularly important for high school students, but at that age the best judgment is sometimes elusive. One group of teenagers decided to broadcast a rather suggestive impression when they discovered they could attract attention with a risqué appearance and a sexy walk. The girls with long eyelashes, heavy makeup, skin-tight blouses, and short skirts seemed to mimic "ladies of the night" on a dark street corner in downtown Toledo. They moved with exaggerated emphasis to shake their body parts with the best curves. The label "street walkers" was quickly assigned to them, and it stuck with members of that group through high school and beyond. Once the impression you communicate creates your brand name, the imagery can follow you for a very long time.

Forming relationships is a critical life skill that is clarified in teen years and then implemented over a lifetime. However, success is sometimes betrayed by a brief event of misfortune which may have long-term consequences. One older boy was known as "Farty Baker." I never knew the details of how the nickname was formed, although I can imagine the precipitating event. That name has stuck for over four decades and he will probably own it for life, as most people have forgotten his real name. The first impression is not necessarily the one you might want others to remember, but it may last a long time.

Mistaken Impressions

Occasionally we reach a conclusion about others which is not accurate. A wrong impression might occur for various reasons, but a mistaken perception can steer decisions in the wrong direction.

There are purchases over the years which I chose without completely understanding the thought process. Successful deliberations, especially those of significant purchases, create a positive reaction which is reinforced each time we enjoy the product of a correct decision, a valid impression. Mistakes like choosing a cheap brand of strawberry jam quickly fade from thought, but costly errors commit an impression to long-term memory. On those occasions that we arrive at a faulty impression, we learn to adjust our perception strategy.

Wrong Impression of a Co-Worker

My first real job, a part-time position in the produce department at Meyer Market, was a great opportunity to begin my work life at the young age of fourteen. As I reflect on that first job at the grocery store, it was easy for me to demonstrate a positive work ethic in the enjoyable work environment. The hours were short, the work was not difficult, and coworkers were entertaining. Walter, the elderly founder of the store, always had something colorful to say. Marv, Walter's son and the owner during my employment, had a dry but ever-present sense of humor. Scott, the owner's fifteen year-old son, liked to clown around. He worked at the meat counter and often swallowed a raw oyster just to see the reaction on people's faces.

Scott was viewed as a comic and a bit on the ornery side, but he made even the difficult work seem like an opportunity to have fun. The store was closed on Sundays, so that was the best day of the week to complete the monthly ritual of cleaning grease off the meat cooler floor. The only way to accomplish the job was to scrape the grease by hand while kneeling on the floor. Scott's humor allowed the time to pass quickly and made the work proceed efficiently. Since only Scott and a coworker were in the store during that strenuous effort, a couple of sodas would usually come up missing during the task. Anyway, the job was successfully completed in a timely fashion. The person with an entertaining impression was not only likable, but truly motivational. Because Scott was a bit naughty, his contribution toward productivity was never quite appreciated by those who focused on his mischief rather than his effort. Theirs was a mistaken perception, though, as they overlooked the valuable impact of his motivational impression.

Entering the Chapel

Whether we realize it or not, we all judge the personalities of people we meet and the places we see and those judgments do affect our decisions.[6] Therefore, the validity of perceptions has consequences. The measuring stick for our impressions is the accuracy of predictions.[7] The test of whether an impression has been accurately perceived and correctly applied is the success or failure of decisions which rely upon the impression.

First Impression of the Chapel

My good friends began to examine the church they had entered. By now their eyes had adjusted to the indoor lighting and they could focus well enough to read posters on the wall and to notice pamphlets on a nearby shelf. There were rosaries on a table for guests to borrow and information regarding vocation activities and mission topics which were available to be delivered by the Fathers of Mercy. Visitors were greeted by a statue of the Blessed Virgin holding the infant Jesus, portrayed as if giving a blessing.[8]

Straining his eyes to the left and to the right, Pete turned to Julie and whispered, "I'm really glad we stopped at that fast food restaurant, because I don't see a restroom nearby." He continued, "I was hoping there would be one here."

"You won't find a restroom in the vestibule back at Sacred Heart Church, either," Julie responded, "but I am sure they have one here in case you need it later. Actually, we may as well plan on you needing one before we leave."

Pete scowled at Julie, but decided not to waste his breath on a reply. He thought to himself, "Even if you win the battle, you will lose the war."

Lasting Impression Inspiration

Sandy turned to Alice and asked, "What was the connection between Larry and the Fathers of Mercy priests?"

Alice replied, "It began with the mission talks a couple of years ago where Larry first met Father George. He actually attended two of the missions in consecutive years, and then began the 'Determining Your Legacy' writing project," she explained. "His connection resumed a couple of years later when he participated in mission talks by Father Louis."

"What do you mean by 'determining your legacy'?" Sandy inquired, as she and Alice stood aside from the others in the vestibule of the Fathers of Mercy Chapel.

"Well, it's a long story," Alice responded. "I think Larry's book was inspired by a trip to Washington, DC. I am sure he could tell the story much better than I can do it, but I'll try."

"As a faculty member at Northwest State Community College, Larry attended a grant meeting at the Department of Education in Washington, DC. Larry had toured most major attractions of the capital years earlier during a high school class trip, but it was his first experience with the newer exhibits. He knew the World War II Memorial had been completed that spring in 2004, but wasn't exactly sure where to find it. Larry asked a National Park Service employee for directions to the World War II Memorial."

"I tell you what," the park ranger had replied. "I could try to explain, but it's hard to describe, so I'll just lead you there."

Alice continued, "Although it was a hot, humid day, the Park Service employee led Larry across the lawn with many turns left and right. Finally, they arrived at the World War II Memorial.

Larry offered to give a tip or buy the man a cold drink, but he refused."

"No, no," the worker replied, "I can't accept that, but what you can do is to give a homeless person a dollar for me whenever you see him."

"With that request, the Park Service employee had made a quick impression and Larry was confident that he had witnessed the man's compassion in just one chance encounter," Alice continued. "That first impression was the inspiration for Larry's book, 'Determining Your Legacy'. We couldn't have known at the time that his writing would lead to this memorial service."

First impressions can have a powerful influence!

---

[1] Susan Fee, "Make a Positive First Impression," *Training & Development* 59, no. 4 (2005), 14.

[2] Monica J. Harris and Christopher P. Garris, "You Never Get a Second Chance to Make a First Impression: Behavioral Consequences of First Impressions," in *First Impressions*, ed. Nalini Ambady & John J. Skowronski (New York: The Guilford Press, 2008), 148.

[3] Carlin Flora, "The Once-Over: Can You Trust First Impressions?" *Psychology Today* 37, no. 3 (2004): 60.

[4] Malcolm Gladwell, *Blink: The Power of Thinking Without Thinking* (New York: Little, Brown, and Company, 2005), 34.

[5] Benita J. Walton-Moss and others, "Risk Factors for Intimate Partner Violence and Associated Injury Among Urban Women," *Journal of Community Health 30*, no. 5 (2005): 377–389.

[6] David C. Funder, "Accurate Personality Judgment," *Current Directions in Psychological Science* 21, no. 3 (2012): 177-182.

[7] Ibid., 178.

[8] Ibid.

Chapter 3
Speed of Impressions

"Did you know that within seconds of meeting someone for the first time, your appearance, body language, and non-verbal communication will create a lasting first impression?"[1]

– N. Jamal and J. Lindenberger

At the Chapel in Kentucky, other conversations sprang up as the weary travelers became better acquainted with each other and their surroundings. They had arrived early with enough time to talk for a few minutes and to appreciate the unique setting.

"Larry didn't seem to mind when I couldn't understand the meaning of lasting impressions," Louie admitted to Wally.

"I know what you mean," Wally replied. "It took me a few chapters to catch on. I did enjoy the stories, and then the true message began to unfold. I was quickly impacted by the effect of impressions we communicate, our legacy for others."

Flashback – Fast Impressions

As my friends discussed my book, I recalled impressions that hit me very quickly earlier in life. My high school senior class trip to New York City and Washington, DC was one of those events that formed a fast impression. Students from rural northwest Ohio rarely traveled to a large city. Since we had free time in New York, three of us discussed what we might do.

First Taxi Ride

"Have you ever ridden in a taxi cab?" I asked. When the others both shook their heads, I suggested, "Let's take a ride!"

Bill replied, "That's a great idea!"

We walked to the curb and waved to the next taxi coming down the street. When he pulled over, the three of us hopped into the yellow cab and Tony yelled, "Follow that car!"

Tires squealed as we were quickly launched into the flow of traffic. We all laughed with delight as we enjoyed the exhilaration of the ride. After only a few blocks, Tony told the driver, "That's far enough. We'll get out here."

The driver was obviously unhappy, but I had no clue what he muttered in an unfamiliar language between English swear words. When I methodically counted out exactly the dollars and cents displayed on the meter, he swore again. That was the first taxi ride for three boys from rural northwest Ohio, and we quickly perceived a negative impression of city transportation. The car was beat up, the driver was rude, his driving was reckless, and the fare was expensive. It is accurate to say that we reached a quick impression of city taxi drivers, and I believe our driver also formed a quick impression of inexperienced country teenagers.

We Form Impressions Quickly

People form first impressions spontaneously, immediately, and with minimal effort of thinking.[2] For years it has been known that first impression memories occur extremely fast. You might recall people whose impact left a fast impression. In retrospect, it is almost comical that we can quickly rush to judgment based upon a single event. I recall a baseball game in which a rookie player hit a home run in his first major league at bat. A fan two seats away quickly declared, "We now have a new slugger."

The image is quickly committed to memory, even though it is exactly one success. I have read the advice of economists, that "one event in a row is not a trend." However, we seem to have a human need to quickly fill the void of judgment any time we might not have an existing opinion. Therefore, a first impression becomes our immediate belief and, whether right or wrong, quickly defines our assessment of people.

Quick Impressions of Young Tourists

In the summer after my high school graduation, I experienced the speed of impressions during a cross-country trip with two of my close friends, Bill and Jon. We drove my father's 1964 Chevy Biscayne sedan with many miles already on the odometer. The only planned events on our itinerary were that: 1) we were driving to the Rocky Mountains and 2) we planned on returning to Ohio ten days later. The rest of the trip would be spontaneous as to where we went, when we arrived, and what we did along the way.

My favorite memory is our crossing over the mountains from Wyoming into Montana, where we stopped for the night in Billings. Although forty years have passed, I recall the trip like it happened yesterday. We had no clue how difficult that journey would become, or the impressions we would encounter on the way.

We had enjoyed two days in Yellowstone National Park, then chose Montana as our next destination. Our map showed a highway heading out the northeast entrance of Yellowstone would deliver us to Billings. As flatlanders from northwest Ohio, we knew nothing about elevation. I later discovered that our route to Billings is the Beartooth American Road, an extremely curvy and scenic highway by daytime. We happened to embark after dusk, negotiating the treacherous Beartooth Pass at an elevation of 11,000 feet in total darkness. After a nail-biting drive on "the highest elevation highway in the northern Rockies", and dozens of hairpin curves with fatal drop-offs, we descended from the mountains and entered Billings, Montana. [3] We were physically tired, emotionally drained, and fiercely hungry.

After checking into a small hotel, we walked next door to a restaurant. The three of us hardly spoke as we scanned the menu. I don't recall what I ordered, but I will never forget the choices of my companions. Jon ordered the trout, which could be seen lying on a customer's plate at the next table with head and eyeballs still intact. Bill chose a BLT sandwich, and then the fun began.

The waitress asked him, "Do you want that on toast?" as she held a pen and notepad.

Bill raised his eyebrows and glared over his glasses as he slowly responded, "Yes."

The girl scribbled on her paper and then asked, "Would you like lettuce on that?"

This time I watched Bill's lips tighten into a frown, his arms folded in front of his chest, and he sternly answered in a louder, slower voice, "Yes!"

At that point I could see exactly where the conversation was headed. A voice in my mind was begging the girl, "Please don't say it! Don't ask the question!"

Sure enough, after writing again, the waitress began to ask, "Would you like tomato . . ."

Before she could finish, Bill jumped to his feet, raised both arms in the air, and screamed, "JUST WHAT THE HELL DO YOU THINK A BLT IS?"

The waitress had unknowingly reinforced the longstanding impression of a young blonde and Bill had just created the funniest impression I can recall during our lifelong friendship. I just know that somewhere in Billings, Montana, patrons are still retelling the story of young tourists who quickly and loudly disrupted the late evening meal in a small local restaurant. I am confident the three of us had left an immediate and vivid impression.

Fast Impressions

Most impressions are formed very quickly. A study by a management consultant, Leonor Cervera, revealed that 62 % of interviewers knew their hiring decision in the first fifteen minutes of a job interview.[4] A recent survey by Accountemps, a division of Robert Half International, also found that job applicants have little time to impress. A majority of human resource professionals form a positive or negative assessment of job applicants in less than ten minutes.[5] An expert in employee hiring processes, Mary Mitchell, promotes the value of developing a quick impression, as she coaches clients that the first five minutes are critical.[6]

Sometimes the future prospects of a relationship can be defined within just a few minutes.[7] In a study of college freshmen, pairs of students met each other on the first day of class and talked for only a few minutes. Students were later asked to complete a questionnaire designed to identify how well they liked their new acquaintance. The students attended multiple classes with each other and were readministered a second survey nine weeks into the term. Students who had given their partner a positive rating at the first meeting were more likely to sit closer and talk more often with the other student. Those who indicated a negative perception in the first survey distanced themselves during later weeks. Not only were impressions during initial conversations correlated with later behavior, it was discovered that three minutes was enough time for students to determine their impressions of each other.

A Job Too Good To Be True

Toward the end of my sophomore year in college, recruiters met with students at Bowling Green State University to enlist them as book salesmen. "You will sell books in Daytona Beach for the summer," they told us. Well, I had already visited Daytona Beach and that sounded great to me, so I signed on with them. After

31

classes ended that spring, I drove to Nashville for a week of sales training. I learned the sales pitch, how to record book orders, and how to counter every reason a customer might refuse to buy. I became familiar with all the books in the sales kit. On Friday we met individually with the staff, who informed me they didn't need all of us in Daytona Beach after all. My new territory was the area surrounding Moncks Corner, South Carolina.

I packed my bags, gathered up my sales kit, and hit the road for the prearranged house I was to rent in Moncks Corner. On my first day, I discovered a great deal of poverty and few willing book buyers. By Tuesday I learned there were swamps between houses and few roads in the countryside. On the third day, I called upon my training to fight off a mean dog with the sales kit, only to discover that the tactic does not work when three dogs attack simultaneously. Day four led me to think the good people of South Carolina did not truly appreciate a Yankee, especially one who wanted to take their money. On Friday, after twice staring down the barrel of a shotgun, I was fairly confident they were not impressed by a young book salesman from Ohio.

By the end of the first week, I had actually sold seven books to people who really could not afford them, but had been convinced by my sales pitch. Because we were not to sell books on Sunday, I took myself out for breakfast to reconsider my career as a door-to-door book salesman.

I convinced myself that it was just a bad week and that I had probably seen the worst of the experience. I spent a second week trying my best to sell books in the Moncks Corner area, but with worse results than the previous week. That second Saturday I packed my car, handed my sales to another poor college student, and drove nonstop to northwest Ohio. For the remainder of the summer I was the most appreciative employee on the payroll at Campbell Soup Company, a job I considered a blessing.

Even at nineteen years old, I could see that a group of college students had been deceived into becoming booksellers. Those recruiters knew that they didn't need hundreds of students to sell books in Daytona Beach. I had experienced firsthand that impressions are difficult to read, but I had quickly seen through their ruse that tricked a group of inexperienced students.

Faster Impressions

Evidence has revealed that it may not take even minutes to form impressions. "Within seconds of meeting you, based on a single observed physical trait or behavior, people will assume to know everything about you."[8] In some cases it has been discovered that people form an opinion of strangers within a minute and a half. "What happens in those 90 seconds can determine whether we succeed or fail at achieving rapport."[9]

A recent study determined that it took only sixty seconds for perceivers to judge strangers, while some contend that it doesn't take even one minute to form an impression.[10]

A Quick Hiring Decision

"You have to go to Campbell's!" my close friend, Kirk, telephoned to let me know. "There is a great summer job opportunity as a salaried employee in the security section."

So, one early spring afternoon I drove through the main gate at Campbell Soup Company, parked my car, and followed the sign up the sidewalk to the "Personnel Office."

George, the hiring manager, stated, "Well, Kirk already told me you're a teacher. Educators are good at paperwork and they go to work each day. I think you could do the job, but let's see what the boss thinks." George led me to Mr. Corbin, Head of Security.

I had hardly entered Mr. Corbin's office, when he asked, "Do you teach night classes?"

"Yes," I responded. "I've had an evening class two nights each week for a year."

"Our guards work all shifts, including mornings, afternoons, and nights," Mr. Corbin stated. "Can you remember faces?"

I replied, "I learn faces and names of 150 students in the first week each term."

"You're hired!" Mr. Corbin shouted. "The last guard misspelled my name, reported late three days in a row, and missed a freight train when it pulled twelve box cars out of the gate only 32 feet away in broad daylight. If you can beat him, you will make it. How soon can you start?"

"I guess right away," I answered. "Thank you very much." I shook Mr. Corbin's hand.

As we walked away, George announced, "Report for a physical exam tomorrow at 8:00 am. That is the last step to become a guard at Campbell Soup Company this summer."

My impression on the interviewers had been quick and successful. After a brief conversation, I left for the day, happy to be hired and contemplating a fast impression of my new boss and the hiring process at Campbell Soup Company.

Even Faster Impressions

"In face-to-face interactions, appearance is the first piece of information available to others."[11] Since the perception of physical appearance is immediate, observers are quickly impacted. Evidence has confirmed that important decisions are chosen after brief encounters. "The psychologists are finding that in some cases our social intuition is indeed amazing - we can sometimes pick up a remarkable amount of information about a person's personality or skills in just a few seconds."[12] We then act on those impressions just as quickly as we formed them.

One researcher measured brain activity created by encounters with strangers. When a group of men and women were shown forty photos in a rapid series, an immediate spike in brain activity was observed for each photo of an attractive person. Results were interpreted by concluding that snap judgments of people occurred within just four seconds of viewing the pictures, as responses were automatic.[13] People are destined to form impressions quickly as an instinct to judge intentions of others and determine appropriate responses.

A New Kindergarten Student

When our son, Shawn, began kindergarten, he had reservations about walking into the building on the first day of school. He really did not want to be there. Our three year-old daughter, Shari, would have gladly traded places with him, but he had to stay instead of her. Throughout the day I thought about how reluctant Shawn had been and I was concerned to learn how his first day of school had gone.

Shawn stepped off the afternoon bus and I asked, "So, how was your first day of school?"

"Great!" he replied, "That Mrs. Arvay is the best teacher!" I had to chuckle at the response. In subsequent years, I learned that Mrs. Arvay truly is a very effective teacher. However, I found it comical that Shawn would declare the first teacher he had ever experienced to be the very best teacher after only one day of observation and with no other teachers for comparison. Such is the speed of a first impression, even the perception of a five year-old.

Still Faster Impressions

Recent studies have shown that trustworthiness is determined visually at a rate faster than conscious processing in the brain. A fraction of a second has proven sufficient to read a stranger's face.

Observers who viewed pictures rated faces on a scale of least threatening to most threatening based on the photos in less than four hundredths of a second.[14] Choices were determined as quickly as facial detection occurred, which indicates decisions were immediately possible. Judgments are not only fast and accurate, but humans reach conclusions faster than they are consciously aware they are making them.

Emotions change facial appearance in milliseconds and expressions are immediately perceived by viewers. Responses are interpreted because human evolution has taught us to recognize when to sense danger, and if we should be prepared to run. Author Paul Ekman calls these "autoappraisers", or automatic-appraising mechanisms, which process visual cues directly from the eyes to the brain without conscious thinking.[15]

The "F" Word

My mother would often watch our children for us when Alice and I went out for the evening. On one occasion, when Shawn was six years old and Shari was four, they were playing in the front room while my mother was in the kitchen. In the middle of her cooking, my mother was interrupted when Shari burst into the room.

"Grandma, grandma, Shawn said the 'F' word, he said the 'F' word!" she shouted.

My mother immediately dropped her spoon into the bowl of ingredients and stomped out of the kitchen with Shari in her wake. She confronted Shawn right where he stood in the middle of the living room.

"What did you say?" grandma asked.

"He said the 'F' word, he said the 'F' word!" Shari answered for him.

Shawn just stared straight ahead, ignoring the question.

"I want to know what you said!" my mother insisted.

He pressed his lips tightly together, standing as still as a statue, staring off into space, and ignoring his grandmother.

"He said the 'F' word!" Shari announced.

"Tell me what you said!" my mother pressed him.

"Okay," Shawn finally responded, "I said 'Fart'."

My mother dropped into a nearby chair, as relief poured over her. Tension was replaced by humor and she burst into laughter.

"I told you Shawn said the 'F' word!" Shari insisted.

When we returned home, my mother explained the story. We all enjoyed a good laugh and were pleased with the way the situation had turned out.

"Actually, Shari was right," I commented, "Shawn did speak a word which begins with the letter 'F'. I am just surprised Shari knew that it was a word that began with an 'F' at only four years of age." Shari's conclusion was a quick assessment of the situation.

Immediate Impressions

We quickly decide if a person deserves a second look. Traits are inferred spontaneously and decisions which utilize the information are determined automatically.[16] The ability to effortlessly judge a person "serves as an initial pass that may determine the likelihood of seeking additional information (i.e., whether to approach or avoid a given individual)."[17]

A "personality judgment instinct" accounts for proficiency in personality judgments among children as well as adults.[18] Malcolm Gladwell has labeled the area of the brain which jumps to immediate conclusions the "adaptive unconscious" because those decisions are reached without conscious thought.[19] "Specific aspects of human cognition may have evolved that facilitate detection of, and defensive responses to, potential harm doers."[20]

It would seem that an observer would need adequate time to consider the type of impression viewed when encountering a stranger. "Instead, as soon as subjects could detect an object at all, they already knew its category."[21] This immediate determination without conscious processing in the brain is consistent with magnetic resonance imaging (MRI) research of brain activity. The entire process of judging a new acquaintance was observed to alter brain waves within two hundredths of a second (seventeen ms).[22]

This indicates that people make judgments automatically, with facial appearance impressions impacting the observer faster than conscious thinking can occur. In one study specific areas of the brain showed immediate neural responses, indicating that "faces are spontaneously evaluated on trustworthiness."[23] In other words once we see an image, we judge it. "Since light travels faster than sound, you are seen before you are heard."[24] Many impressions are formed in the blink of an eye at first sight.

Fast Impressions of the Chapel

"I'm really glad we can be here to show our support for Larry," Louie stated. "So this is the Chapel in Kentucky where Larry came several times?" he asked.

"Yes, this is where he came to visit his friends, Father George and Father Louis," Alice answered. "It is a longer drive than I expected." After a moment of silence, she then suggested, "Well, shall we enter the Chapel and find a seat?"

As the group stepped forward, they read the motto of the Fathers of Mercy stenciled above the Chapel doorway, "He was moved with mercy" (from Luke 15:20).[25] Crossing the threshold, all were struck with awe as they inhaled the aura of the ornate Chapel. The dim interior was silent, almost mysterious at this early hour. Rows of mahogany pews complemented the pattern in the marble floor and, after appreciating the elegance of the layout, eyes were drawn up the huge columns toward the high ceiling with extensive stenciling of red paint and gold leafing.

Hesitating long enough for some members of the group to reach for the holy water and then make the sign of the cross, they began the deliberate journey down the center aisle. It was difficult for them to focus on the walkway, each foot slowly and steadily placed in front of the other as their attention was drawn left and right to gaze toward the outer walkways. Every few feet an illuminated alcove interrupted the design of the outside aisles where each indentation in the wall was an arch which outlined the large, intricately carved statue of a prominent saint. Most were easily identified, as each figure is positioned in a scene which represented an event from their lives of service on earth.

The group stopped midway down the aisle to look upward once again, where an angel was painted above each of the ten columns of the Chapel, five on either side. Each angel held a tablet inscribed with one of the Ten Commandments. Above the angels on the left was a banner which read, "For the sake of his sorrowful passion, have mercy on us and on the whole world."[26] A painted banner on the right side of the nave was inscribed, "Holy God, Holy Mighty One, Holy Immortal One have mercy on us and on the whole world."[27] The inscriptions, taken from the Chaplet of Divine Mercy prayer, embrace all who visit. Twelve stained glass windows above the inscriptions, six on each side, display a symbol of a special event in the life of each of the Apostles.

Closer to the front of the church were several wooden confessionals which had been built into the walls on both sides of the Chapel and had been hand carved to match the design of the seating. Small wooden doors for penitents left little doubt of the purpose of such rooms in a Catholic Church. The peaceful, reverent scene provided a perfect opportunity for reflection.

The party of friends resumed their slow journey forward, deliberately placing one foot before the other as they stared intently at the scenes on both sides of the church. It was easy to see beyond the rows of pews to fully appreciate the entire scene, as few people were seated this early. Overall, visitors to the Chapel perceived a decidedly welcoming impression.

"Isn't this an amazing scene?" Alice asked Sandy.

"I am immediately impressed that this is an inspiring place," Sandy replied.

Alice answered, "Larry had told me of a quote that said people can quickly size up a situation within seconds and then reach a fast impression."[28] "I guess we are also quickly forming an impression during our visit for this memorial service."

"Isn't this a remarkable story that brought us here today?" Pete asked.

"It is quite an amazing impact explained in Larry's book," Wally concurred. "I'm glad we are able to be here to honor Larry and the exclamation point on a life lived for others."

We often form impressions very quickly!

---

[1] Nina Jamal and Judith Lindenberger, "How to Make a Great First Impression," *Business Knowhow*, accessed December 29, 2011, http://www.businessknowhow.com/growth/dress-impression.htm.

[2] Nalini Ambady, Mark Hallahan, and Robert Rosenthal, "On Judging and Being Judged Accurately in Zero-Acquaintance Situations," *Journal of Personality and Social Psychology* 69 (1995): 518-529; Donal E. Carlston and John J. Skowronski, "Linking Versus Thinking: Evidence for the Different Associative and Attributional Bases of Spontaneous Trait Transference and Spontaneous Trait Inference," *Journal of Personality and Social Psychology* 89 (2005): 884-898; Christopher Olivola and Alexander Todorov, "Fooled by First Impressions? Reexamining the Diagnostic Value of Appearance-Based Inferences," *Journal of Experiential Social Psychology* 46 (2010): 315-324; Lea Winerman, "'Thin Slices' of Life," *Monitor on Psychology* 36, no. 3 (2005):54.

[3] Friends of the Beartooth All-American Road, "On the Wild Side of Yellowstone", accessed March 16, 2013, http://www.beartoothhighway.com/wildRoad/index.html.

[4] Leonor Cervera, "First Impressions Count," *USA Today*, Sept. 19, 1988.

[5] Chad Brooks, "10 Minutes Is All Employers Need to Evaluate Job Candidates, " last modified September 19, 2012, http://www.cnbc.com/id/49087046/10_Minutes_Is_All_Employers_Need_to_E valuate_Job_Candidates.

[6] Mary Mitchell, *The First Five Minutes: How to Make a Great First Impression in AnyBusiness Situation* (New York: John Wiley & Sons, Inc., 1998).

[7] Michael Sunnafrank and Artemio Ramirez, "At First Sight: Persistent Relational Effects of Get-Acquainted Conversations," *Journal of Social and Psychological Relationships* 21, no. 3 (2004): 361-379.

[8] H. Andrew Michener, John D. DeLamater, and Daniel J. Myers. *Social Psychology* (Belmont, CA: Wadsworth, 2003).

[9] Nicholas Boothman, *How to Make People Like You in 90 Seconds or Less* (New York: Workman, 2003), 28.

[10] Nalini Ambady, Mary Anne Krabbenhoft, and Daniel Hogan, "The 30-Sec Sale: Using Thin-Slice Judgments to Evaluate Sales Effectiveness," *Journal of Consumer Psychology* 16, no. 1 (2006): 4-13.

[11] Laura P. Naumann and others, "Personality Judgments Based on Physical Appearance," *Personality and Social Psychology Bulletin* 35, no. 12 (2009): 1661.

[12] Lea Winerman, "'Thin Slices' of Life," *Monitor on Psychology* 36, no. 3 (2005): 54.

[13] Ibid., p. 66.

[14] Moshe Bar, Maital Neta, and Heather Linz, "Very First Impressions," *Emotion* 6, no. 2 (2006): 269-278.

[15] Paul Ekman, *Emotions Revealed: Recognizing Faces and Feelings to Improve Communication and Emotional Life* (New York: Owl Books, Henry Holt and Company, LLC., 2003), 21.

[16] Randy J. McCarthy and John J. Skowronski, "What Will Phil Do Next? Spontaneously Inferred Traits Influence Predictions of Behavior," *Journal of Experimental Social Psychology* 47, (2011): 321-332; Matthew T. Crawford and others, "Inferences Are For Doing: The Impact of Approach and Avoidance States on the Generation of Spontaneous Trait Inferences," *Personality and Social psychology Bulletin* 39, no. 3, (2013): 267-278; Randy J. McCarthy and John J. Skowronski, "The Interplay of Controlled and Automatic Processing in the Expression of Spontaneously Inferred Traits: A PDP Analysis," *Journal of Personality and Social Psychology* 100, no. 2 (2011): 229-240.

41

[17] Matthew T. Crawford and others, "Inferences Are For Doing: The Impact of Approach and Avoidance States on the Generation of Spontaneous Trait Inferences," *Personality and Social Psychology Bulletin* 39, no. 3, (2013): 267-278; Randy J. McCarthy and John J. Skowronski, "The Interplay of Controlled and Automatic Processing in the Expression of Spontaneously Inferred Traits: A PDP Analysis," *Journal of Personality and Social Psychology* 100, no. 2 (2011): 275.

[18] Martie G. Haselton and David C. Funder, "The Evolution of Accuracy and Bias in Social Judgment," In *Evolution and Social Psychology,* eds. Mark Schaller, Jeffry A. Simpson, and Douglas T. Kenrick (New York: Psychology Press, 2006), 15-37.

[19] Malcolm Gladwell, *Blink: The Power of Thinking Without Thinking* (New York: Little, Brown, and Company, 2005), 11.

[20] Ibid., p. 16.

[21] Kalanit Grill-Spector and Nancy Kanwisher, "Visual Recognition: As Soon As You Know It Is There, You Know What It Is," *Psychological Science* 16, no. 2 (2005): 158.

[22] Kalanit Grill-Spector, Nicholas Knouf, and Nancy Kanwisher, "The Fusiform Face Area Sub Serves Face Perception, Not Generic Within-Category Identification," *Nature Neuroscience* 7 (2004): 555-562.

[23] Alexander Todorov, Sean G. Baron, and Nickolaas N. Oosterhof, "Evaluating Face Trustworthiness: A Model Based Approach," *Social Cognitive and Affective Neuroscience* 3, no. 2 (2008): 126.

[24] Nina Jamal and Judith Lindenberger, "How to Make a Great First Impression," *Business Knowhow*, accessed December 29, 2011, http://www.businessknowhow.com/growth/dress-impression.htm.

[25] United States Conference of Catholic Bishops, *The New American Bible* (Washington: United States Conference of Catholic Bishops, 2002), 1119.

[26] Fr. Louis Guardiola, *The Catechetical Tour of The Divine Mercy Chapel of The Fathers of Mercy of The Immaculate Conception of the Blessed Virgin Mary of South Union, Kentucky* (Auburn, KY: The Fathers of Mercy, 2013), 14.

[27] Ibid.

[28] Camille Lavington, *You've Only Got Three Seconds: How to Make the Right Impression in YourBusiness and Social Life* (New York: Doubleday, 1998), 1.

Chapter 4
Accuracy of Impressions

"First impressions are often the truest."[1] – William Hazlitt

As my closest friends entered the Fathers of Mercy Chapel, I could see their curious looks as they wondered why I had been attracted to this setting. I was not entirely certain myself, except I know it was the one place that most inspired me. There is an ambience about the Chapel which is peaceful and inspirational, that seems simultaneously timeless and timely.

My long-time friends continued their walk down the center aisle of the Chapel. Soon their main focus was on side altars to the left and right, as well as the Altar of Sacrifice in the middle. The adjacent altars held familiar statues of Mary and Joseph amid an intricate design, while the High Altar held the gilded tabernacle with gold plating and a cross. A marble communion railing extended the width of the Chapel with red padded kneeler, which harkened memories of an earlier era in Catholic churches. Behind the railing on the left and the right, facing the center, were several rows of pews providing nearby seating for multiple celebrants.

As the visitors neared the front of the Chapel, eyes were drawn to a beautiful combination of modern construction and ornate altars. A pulpit with four symbols represents the Gospel authors and carved inscriptions decorate the front of the Altar of Sacrifice. The group viewed a painting of The Divine Mercy in the center of the apse above the high altar. Our Lady of Lourdes, "The Immaculate Conception", is displayed on the right, while the left side has a painting of "The Prodigal Son" kneeling at the feet of his father.[2]

"Somehow this Chapel appears new and traditional at the same time," Pete told the others.

My friend, Pete, was spot on accurate with his impression. While the Chapel is only a few years old, the side altars had been relocated when a historic church in Cincinnati was closed.

Flashback – Accurate Impressions

Pete's correct assessment reminded me of times I have arrived at an accurate impression. Each of us is experienced at interpreting what we see and hear to determine our perception of a new acquaintance. Since we have been so accurate in previous observations, we continue to rely upon our brief assessment of situations when making decisions.

Accurate Impressions of Quality

I had always heard about the favorable reputation of Sauder Manufacturing, but I had not experienced their furniture products until the purchase of chairs for a new building on campus. "If you ever need a testimonial on the quality of your chairs, you can send potential customers out here to the College," I suggested to a manager from Sauder who happened to be on campus. "We bought 240 of your chairs in 1989 and there hasn't been one failure of the frames or fabric in over twenty-seven years. Students are in those chairs hour after hour, day after day, during fall, spring, and summer. As I recall, the chairs didn't cost much more than $100 each. We have gotten our money's worth out of those chairs."

A slow grin came over the manager's face as he replied, "Thank you very much. We are proud of our chairs." He continued, "However, we might have made them too well. You see, we would have preferred to sell you replacement chairs, but they just seem to last forever."

I have seen Sauder chairs in the offices of other organizations since that conversation. The perception of Sauder Manufacturing is one of high quality production and value for the dollar. Quality of workmanship is guaranteed on their website and that is exactly the attention to excellence that I had experienced with the Sauder chairs. The comments I had heard for years were proven to be true by the successful product which accurately validated the positive impression of Sauder Manufacturing. One sure sign of a successful company is a product which exceeds the customer's expectations, reinforcing accuracy of the buyer's impression.

Amazingly Accurate

It is possible to accurately sense intentions of others by mere observation. Most adults are experts in recognizing emotions by viewing the faces of others.[3] By the age of ten, even children are proficient at matching facial expressions with emotions.[4] The ratings of young observers who were shown facial photos of strangers displayed a significant correlation between pictures which expressed a negative emotion and an untrustworthy rating.[5]

Perceptions can be accurately achieved within a single second, as demonstrated by viewers who were shown photos of political candidates they did not know.[6] A one-second exposure to pictures of candidates for national offices was enough time for participants to choose the photo they believed to project the more competent appearance. "After the elections, the researchers compared the competency judgments and election outcomes and found that participants correctly selected winners in 72.4% of senatorial races and 68.6% of gubernatorial contests."[7] First impressions in decision making can be accurately determined in as little as one second of observation during a single encounter.

We often form perceptions quickly and then review them when additional evidence becomes available. In most cases our initial assessment is reinforced, validating the accuracy of the first impression.

Youthful Accurate Conclusions

Our son, Shawn, took me to task when I was elected to the Board of Education for our local school. While a first grader, he complained to me that kids should be allowed to chew gum at school and that I should do something about the number of recesses in grade school.

"When I was in kindergarten we had three recesses, but in first grade there are only two," Shawn explained. "At this rate, pretty soon we won't get any recesses."

Shawn had been exactly right in his prediction. However, I didn't have the heart to tell him those recesses really would disappear in a few years. He would learn that lesson about recesses on his own soon enough.

I was surprised how quickly my grandson, Breyer, stated his impressions from recent food observations when only eight years-old. He had ordered dessert in a restaurant and then complained, "This apple pie doesn't look anything like the menu." He quickly told me, "It's just like baking a frozen pizza that never looks like the picture on the box." Breyer's conclusion was right on target, but I was surprised he could be so accurate at a very young age.

Consensus of Accuracy

Consensus among observers is often found in perceptions of new acquaintances. In a recent study, the accuracy of impressions was identified by finding a high correlation existed between the beliefs of subjects and perceptions by their observers.[8]

Additionally, when multiple observers agree in their perceptions, the interpretations tend to be correct. "In general, perceptions that demonstrate the highest levels of consensus almost always demonstrate the highest levels of agreement"[9] A surprisingly high level of accuracy has been found for viewers whose observations of strangers compared similarly with the impressions of fellow observers. Personalities of 157 subjects in a study were rated by 299 peers who had multiple interactions with them for eighteen months and by 152 strangers who had only observed them on one occasion for five minutes.[10] The strangers were nearly identical in their assessments. Additionally, the peers and strangers were consistent in perceptions of the subjects, leading to a conclusion of accuracy based on their consensus. Essentially, that many people couldn't all be wrong.

Wisconsin Braided Rope

Whenever someone talks about a fishing trip, I am reminded of a Wisconsin trip several years ago. Louie and I flew to Minneapolis, and then we drove to Bill's cabin in northern Wisconsin. As we prepared for the next morning of fishing, Bill explained he had a special rope for the boat without a knot in it.

"It's called a Wisconsin Weave," he stated, "The rope is braided back into itself without tying a knot."

"Yeah, right," Louie replied with skepticism. "I don't care what you call that rope. Just as long as it works, we'll be okay."

The next morning we arose early and headed to the lake. Bill backed the boat trailer into the water, and then Louie tossed me the end of the rope, unhooked the boat from the trailer, and pushed the boat into the water. I pulled on the rope to bring the boat to the bank, but the other end of the cord went limp and fell off of the boat. I grabbed the bow just as the boat was about to float away and pulled it to the shore.

"That's not much of a weave in that rope!" I exclaimed, as we all laughed and climbed into the boat. We went on to enjoy a beautiful sunny day on the lake. After a few beers and a great fish dinner at the local restaurant that evening (we hadn't caught any fish on the lake), we returned to the cabin. Once the boat was gassed and tackle was readied for the next day, we went inside.

After several minutes of reflection, Bill announced, "I figured out why the rope didn't work." He assured us, "It's now ready."

Early the next morning, we hopped in the van for the short drive to the boat launch. As he had done the previous day, Bill backed the vehicle until the boat trailer went into the water. Louie tossed me the end of the rope and then he shoved the unlatched boat into the lake. As I pulled on the rope, it tightened but fell off the boat again. This time I had to step into the water to grab the boat and pull it back to the shore.

"I can't believe it fell off again!" Louie shouted, "Put an Ohio knot on that stupid Wisconsin rope!"

We all enjoyed a good laugh, especially when the other guys saw my wet foot. Once again, we all climbed into the boat and enjoyed a day in the sun, on the water, amid Bald Eagles, and we actually caught a few fish. At the end of the day, we cleaned and gassed the boat, then retired to the cabin.

After a while, Bill informed us, "I have this rope working now. See how well it tightens on itself when I pull on it?"

"I'm not impressed when it works in the cabin," Louie replied, "I want to see that rope work on the boat."

I woke up looking forward to our third morning of fishing. By now it felt like the movie "Groundhog Day" and I just knew that the stupid rope would repeat the same failure again. As the three of us got into the van, Louie and I glanced at each other and snickered. Once again, Bill backed the boat into the water, Louie threw me the end of the rope, and then he shoved the boat out of the trailer. Louie ran to join me at the waterline just as the rope pulled loose from the boat once again.

"I'm not going in after the boat this time," I told him. "It's farther away and I'm not getting wet today."

As the boat began to drift, Louie shouted, "Hand me the rope!" He quickly fashioned a loop and swung it over his head.

"You think you can lasso a boat?" I asked.

Sure enough, he tossed the loop over the motor and pulled the boat backward to the shore. We all climbed in and headed toward deeper water to once again find the fish.

"You're lucky this is our last day," Louie told Bill, "If that rope had failed one more time, I'd throw you in after the boat."

We enjoyed a good laugh and another day on the lake with beautiful scenery and great friends. Although it's been several years, the memory of that weekend stays with me. While the fishing was lousy and the rope was faulty, the conclusion among us was that we had once again celebrated our lifelong friendship. The three of us had reached a consensus regarding the need to celebrate good times and the long-term bond among us which has continued over many years.

Accurate Positive Impressions

According to experts, a positive self-presentation by a new acquaintance leads to more accurate perceptions by observers than the behavior of subjects who present a negative image.[11] It is possible that positive presenters are viewed as more engaging and cause perceivers to pay more attention to them.

Accuracy is also related to genuineness of self-presentations. According to researchers, the popularity of Facebook is enhanced by the honesty of postings.[12] When participants can be trusted, energy is not wasted filtering posts for doubtful information, freeing effort to focus on the processing of impressions. Accuracy has also been tied to quick perceptions. "People who rely on their 'gut reactions' when forming impressions tend to be more

49

accurate."[13] The first impression tends to be valid much like the first answer chosen in a multiple choice test is usually accurate.

Advice to the Groom

My wife and I have attended many wedding receptions at which an opportunity was provided for women to give advice to the bride and men were invited to share wisdom with the groom. When the announcer asked if any guests had wisdom to impart, several people got up from their chairs. I immediately stood and walked confidently to the front of the room. I shook hands with the groom and spoke a few words in his ear. He then nodded with a grin on his face, and I quickly returned to our table.

I could sense that Alice was watching me for some sign of my discussion and listening for a clue as to what I had told the groom, but I purposely ignored her. After a few minutes, my wife could no longer contain her curiosity. She asked, "So just what advice did you think the groom needed to know?"

Her question elicited my quick reply, "I simply told him what every husband needs to know. There are times in life that he will be the only person who knows he's right, and he needs to be okay with that. He will achieve inner peace knowing that wisdom." I don't know if that awareness will comfort him, but my hunch is that he will find my advice to be spot on accurate.

Accuracy with Limited Data

Accuracy of observers has been determined in their ability to predict the performance of strangers. Perceivers have been able to distinguish more successful leaders from less successful ones based on appearance alone.[14] "Thus, participants' naïve impressions of leadership ability from CEO's faces are significantly related to how much profit those CEO's companies make."[15] Accurate perceptions about management skills were possible with no information to consider other than appearance.

Some researchers found that assessments of teachers in one glance formed ratings which were closely correlated with those of students who had observed the teacher for an entire semester.[16] Thus, assessments in just one brief acquaintance were not only fast, but also accurate. "Moreover, judgments based on 30-s exposures (three 10-second clips of each teacher) were not significantly more accurate than judgments based on 6-s exposures (three 2-second clips of each teacher)."[17] Accuracy is often achieved with limited data in short order.

Outsmarted by a Third Grader

My wife, Alice, and I took our two young grandsons, Breyer and Karter, to the town of Grand Rapids, Ohio one summer day to ride an authentic canal boat. The crew in period costume narrated the reenactment of a ride through the channel, using the boat's rudder to carefully steer us through the waterway. A muleskinner led the mule, which pulled the boat with a rope as the animal walked down the towpath. During our passage, the boat was pulled into a restored canal lock and the wooden doors closed behind us. Water poured in and slowly raised the boat four feet. Then the upstream doors opened to allow us to continue.

After a short ride, the boat turned around and retraced our route back into the lock. As the doors closed and water was released, the boat lowered. The downstream doors were opened and we sailed back into the channel, where I noticed a young boy trotting down the sidewalk along the shore adjacent to the boat.

"I want us to beat that kid back to the dock!" Breyer shouted.

"Well, I don't think we can win," I responded. "The mule is walking slowly and this boat won't go any faster than he pulls the rope. There's nothing we can do to beat that kid to the dock."

After a moment, Breyer jumped off his seat and ran to the boat window. He shouted, "Hey Kid! Your mother's calling you!"

The boy stopped dead in his tracks and turned to look for his parent while our boat cruised into the dock in front of him. Breyer had proven me wrong with a creative trick to win the race back to the dock. Within seconds the nine year-old boy had also left an impression of his quick and accurate solution on nearby passengers who enjoyed a hearty laugh.

Accuracy Is Stable

Accuracy of first impressions has not waivered across differences of age, ethnicity, or culture. According to an impression study, judgments of people's emotions were found to be consistent even across twenty different cultures.[18] Accuracy of human perception appears to be stable regardless of geographic residence or cultural background of the perceivers.

In one experiment researchers showed pictures of unknown French political candidates to Swiss citizens, male and female, who promptly selected election winners at a rate greater than random chance.[19] Interestingly, Swiss children ages five to thirteen years viewed candidates and successfully picked the outcomes of elections at a rate which correlated with selections of the adult voters. The ability to choose election outcomes has been found in several other countries as well, including Australia, New Zealand, and the United Kingdom, even when photos from other cultures halfway around the world were presented to observers.[20] It appears that accuracy of impressions through facial observation is universal, and hardly affected by culture, age, or gender.

Start Healthy, Stay Healthy With Gerber

Gerber recently celebrated the eighty-fifth anniversary of commitment to early childhood nutrition.[21] The company began in 1928 when Dorothy and Dan Gerber decided to strain baby food for their seven month-old daughter, Sally. Their kitchen effort quickly grew into the most well-known and respected producer of foods manufactured to meet the nutritional and developmental needs of children up to four years of age.[22]

Gerber is also famous for support of children's causes. The Gerber Foundation has maintained a close relationship with DeVos Children's Hospital in Grand Rapids, Michigan and recently awarded $5 million to assist with a hospital expansion.[23] By the end of 2009, the Gerber Foundation had given more than $65 million in grants over the years.

Parents continue to rely on Gerber to provide healthy food products for their children. Each generation turns to Gerber to satisfy nutrition for infants and their trust is continuously reinforced by high quality foods which provide a nutritionally sound and healthy start for children. The lesson for other companies is that a consistently effective product reinforces consumers' purchase decisions and leads them to validate that their positive perception is an accurate impression.

Seated at the Front of the Chapel

The column of visitors nearly bumped into each other as those at the front came to an abrupt stop. The party of friends stepped out of the aisle, some after genuflecting, and entered the first pew. A few stopped for a brief moment of prayer on the kneeler, and eventually all took a seat. Some checked their watches to see how soon the time would arrive for the service to begin, while others silenced their cell phones to avoid untimely disruptions.

I observed my friends' focus on every detail of their surroundings at the Chapel. They exhibited anticipation for this event like the reaction when awaiting the start of a publicized movie or the initial visit to a newly opened restaurant. As they pointed and nodded in quiet conversations, I could see their appreciation for the beauty and reverence of the setting. Facial expressions told me my friends had accurately reached a favorable impression of the Chapel.

As the group of visitors waited for the memorial to begin at the Chapel, I reflected on the example of that conscientious Park Service employee that I had met years earlier. My book is really a reflection of his inspiration. His lesson has motivated me to think differently when I encounter needy people on street corners in large cities and in small towns.

I used to hesitate when I saw someone asking for assistance, but that National Park Service worker now jumps to the forefront of my memory. Each time I hand over a few dollars, I can't help but think that of that Good Samaritan in Washington, DC. I am also reminded that the generosity of that kind man is contagious and his intention to create concern for others has been fulfilled. Although I will probably never know his name or anything specific about him, that man's values and his good will are his lasting impression on others, as I have experienced for several years.

As my friend, Kirk, sat in the front pew at the Chapel, his eyes scanned from left to right, taking in the ambience of the scene. After a minute, he turned and commented to the others, "We need to leave a donation to help maintain this setting."

"You're right," Dan replied, "Although we may never visit again, I'm sure the priests would appreciate a contribution."

"I'd say it looks like the example of that generous Park Service employee is still making an impression on others," Sandy commented as she smiled.

"That is exactly the kind of reaction people show when the 'lasting impression' story is shared," Alice explained. "Impressions of people really can be accurate and motivating."

"It is really a compliment that the priests would provide this memorial," Sandy replied.

"It is very nice of them to host this service and to share the example of a legacy. The last time we had discussed the book, Larry told me there was more to this story than meets the eye," Alice responded. "He didn't explain, but I suspect we will find out today exactly what that means."

Impressions are often accurate!

[1] William Hazlitt, *Table Talk: Original Essays on Men and Manners* (London: C. Templeman, 1861), 244.

[2] Fr. Louis Guardiola, *The Catechetical Tour of The Divine Mercy Chapel of The Fathers of Mercy of The Immaculate Conception of the Blessed Virgin Mary of South Union, Kentucky* (Auburn, KY: The Fathers of Mercy, 2013), 26.

[3] Derek M. Isaacowitz and others, "Age Differences in Recognition of Emotion in Lexical Stimuli and Facial Expressions," *Psychology and Aging* 22 (2007): 147-159.

[4] Arlene S. Walker-Andrews, "Infants' Perception of Expressive Behaviors: Differentiation of Multimodal Information," *Psychological Bulletin* 121 (1997): 437-456.

[5] Joel S. Winston and others, "Automatic and Intentional Brain Responses During Evaluation of Trustworthiness of Faces," *Nature Neuroscience* 5, no. 3 (2002): 277-283.

[6] Sharon Jayson, "Are Voters Taking Candidates at Face Value?" *USA Today*, Oct. 23, 2007:4D.

[7] Ibid., p. 4D.

[8] David A. Kenny and others, "Consensus at Zero Acquaintance: Replication, Behavioral Cues, and Stability," *Journal of Personality and social Psychology* 62, (1992): 88-97; Peter Borkenau and Anette Liebler, "Trait Inferences: Sources Validity at Zero Acquaintance," *Journal of Personality & Social Psychology* 62 (1992): 645-657; Peter J. Rentfrow and Samuel D. Gosling, "Message in a Ballad: The Role of Music Preferences in Interpersonal Perception," *Psychological Science* 17 (2006): 236-242.

[9] David A. Kenny and Tessa V. West, "Zero Acquaintance: Definitions, Statistical Model, Findings, and Processes," In *First impressions,* eds. Nalini Ambady and John J. Skowronski (New York: The Guilford Press, 2008), 138.

[10] David C. Funder and C. Randall Colvin, "Friends and Strangers: Acquaintanceship, Agreement, and the Accuracy of Personality Judgment," *Journal of Personality and Social Psychology* 55, no. 1 (1988): 149-158.

[11] Lauren J. Human and others, "Your Best Self Helps Reveal Your True Self: Positive Self-Presentation Leads to More Accurate Personality Impressions," *Social Psychological and Personality Science* 3, no. 1 (2012): 23-30.

[12] Mitja D. Back and others, "Facebook Profiles Reflect Actual Personality, Not Self-Idealization," *Psychological Science* 21, no. 3 (2010): 372-374.

[13] Nicholas O. Rule and Nalini Ambady, "The Face of Success," *Psychological Science* 19, no. 2 (2008): 111.

[14] Nicholas O. Rule and Nalini Ambady, "The Face of Success," *Psychological Science* 19, no. 2 (2008): 109-111.

[15] Ibid., p. 110.

[16] Nalini Ambady and Robert Rosenthal, "Half a Minute: Predicting Teacher Evaluations from Thin Slices of Nonverbal Behavior and Physical Attractiveness," *Journal of Personality and Social Psychology* 64, no. 3 (1993): 431-441.

[17] Ibid., p. 438.

[18] Paul Ekman, *Emotions Revealed: Recognizing Faces and Feelings to Improve Communication and Emotional Life* (New York: Owl Books, Henry Holt and Company, LLC, 2003), 21.

[19] John Antonakis and Olaf Dalgas, "Predicting Elections: Child's Play," *Science* 323, no. 5918 (2009): 1183.

[20] Anthony C. Little and others, "Facial Appearance Affects Voting Decisions," *Evolution and Human Behavior* 28, no. 1(2007): 18-27.

[21] "Happy 85th Birthday Gerber!" accessed August 24, 2013, http://news.gerber.com/news/happy-85th-birthday-gerber-let-245121.

[22] "Heritage," accessed August 24, 2013, http://www.gerber.com/AllStages/About/Heritage.aspx.

[23] "The Gerber Foundation," accessed August 24, 2013, http://www.gerberfoundation.org/home/history.

Chapter 5
Longevity of Impressions

"Once that opinion has been formed, it is difficult, if not impossible, for you to change it."[1] – Mary Mitchell

The service at the Fathers of Mercy Chapel began with the playing of a familiar entrance hymn as the procession of celebrants walked slowly up the center aisle. First came three of the brothers, two acolytes carrying candles as they walked on each side of the brother who was the cross bearer. Immediately behind them was one of the priests holding up the book of gospels. Finally the celebrant, Father David, completed the group on a solemn walk toward the altar.

The procession arrived at the communion railing and the brothers halted for a moment while the priests caught up with them, and all stopped for a moment to bow. They resumed walking forward and the candles were then positioned at each side of the front altar. The crucifix was inserted into its brass base. The book of gospels was placed onto the altar, where Father David took his place facing the people.

"Welcome to the Fathers of Mercy Chapel. A memorial service is meant to commit another's deeds to memory," the celebrant explained. "It is our effort to remember one who generously demonstrated charity with his talents and to honor him by improving our lives each time we recall his lasting impression."

Flashback – Stubborn Impressions

Impressions are often committed to memory, even fixed in time. I remember a World War II veteran who was determined to go to his grave without ever purchasing a Japanese product. Some of my friends are diehard fans of Notre Dame football, basketball, and anything Irish and have remained that way for fifty years. Some impressions are truly long-term. You might reflect on opinions that you can recall which are firmly entrenched, such as drinkers of Pepsi or Coca-Cola who are completely loyal to their preference.

Our beliefs are sometimes carved in stone, as we are all prone to rely on information which supports our views and we are likely to ignore facts which conflict. It is quicker and easier when we hold onto an opinion which we can simply recall in later situations rather than taking the time to reconsider our initial perception.

Attitudes are not easily changed, even when later information contradicts an earlier impression. Initial evaluations tend to last a long time, in spite of additional new information which may not agree.[2] The presence of conflicting observations, even the revelation of false information, will not always overcome initial perceptions.

The discovery of more accurate information does not necessarily persuade jurors to change their earlier impressions which had been formed from faulty details about the accused in criminal proceedings.[3] "In general, participants appeared to have been unable to overcome their initial impression of untrustworthiness of the accused, and interpreted evidence in such a way as to reinforce their initial impression."[4] There is an inertia which surrounds a first impression that requires an extraordinary effort to move the perception in favor of new information.

I Hired the "Better Qualified Candidate"

I can still recall a 1995 segment of "Dateline NBC" in which employers were videotaped as they interviewed job applicants.[5] The appearance of some candidates had been purposely embellished, while the looks of others were diminished. Resumes of applicants included identical education and experience. Although each candidate presented the same paper credentials, the more attractive candidate was hired in every case whether the process involved males or females.

Each employer asked the more handsome applicant, "How soon can you start?"

"We might call you in a few weeks," employers told the less attractive candidate.

When confronted with the video and copies of applicant resumes, each employer tried to claim that the attractive applicant they had selected was the "better qualified candidate." Even a playing of the recorded evidence did not sway their story and a review of identical paper documents could not convince them that the qualifications were equal. Their first impression of applicants, biased as it was, could not be changed, as they went to great lengths to rationalize the hiring decision afterward.

Some Impressions are Nearly Permanent

According to first impression authors Ann Demarais and Valerie White, "psychological research has shown that people weigh initial information much more heavily than later information when they evaluate people. In other words, people are more likely to believe that the first things they learn are the truth."[6] The impact of one early negative event requires many positive experiences in future encounters to overcome it, and in some cases the perception may not change even then.

It has also been determined that expectations are maintained in the face of contradictory evidence.[7] Successful performance by those viewed as likeable is often attributed to their genuine abilities, while success by unliked individuals is often discredited as a lucky outcome. Conversely, poor performance by popular people tends to be blamed on others or due to some uncontrollable factor, while negative behavior by unliked persons is deemed to be genuine and consistent with their personal faults. "The end result, from the point of view of the perceiver, is that the original impression still appears to be accurate."[8]

As consumers, we can be influenced by an effective marketing jingle which sticks with us and steers our purchases. However, positive encounters also stay in memory. Over a long term of purchase experiences, a reliable brand becomes our first choice. The consistent integrity of products and services determines the level of consumer confidence regarding future decisions.

Longevity of the Procter & Gamble Impression

Children have observed parents' shopping patterns in the grocery store and reliance on brand-name household cleaners for many years. Generations have passed along the confidence in Procter & Gamble as the producer of preferred products for families since 1837. "P & G brands serve about 4.8 billion of the nearly seven billion people on the planet today."[9] The company sells products in 180 countries and the current workforce represents 150 nationalities.

Procter & Gamble received numerous awards over the years, recently ranked thirteenth among "America's Most Reputable Companies" and number forty-one in the world (Forbes). They were rated number fifteen among the "World's Most Admired Companies" and second in their industry (Fortune). Procter & Gamble was selected first among the "40 Best Companies for Leaders" (Chief Executive Magazine) and number twenty-one on the "World's Most Respected Companies List" (Barron's). Their diversity record is rated eighth in the world (Diversity, Inc.) and P & G is one of the "Top 10 Companies for Executive Women" (National Association for Female Executives).[10]

For more than 175 years, families have relied on the quality of Procter & Gamble products with unwavering confidence. With over 70 brands of beauty, grooming, and household care products, P & G serves almost every household in America. Their reputation is based on the long-term impression of quality. Other businesses would be wise to learn that a long-term reputation leads to longevity of customer loyalty.

We Don't Always Know Why We Believe What We Believe

We often commit an impression to memory without knowing how or why it was formed. People are sometimes not consciously aware of the impact of previous influences and may not be able to determine impressions objectively.[11] As they are not aware of a possible bias from an earlier impression, they do not recognize the need to correct their earlier erroneous assessment.

A recent study documented the longevity of initial impressions, including many which were inaccurate.[12] Observers drew inferences about subjects and then later discovered that information at the heart of their perceptions had been bogus. Although the truth had been revealed, the initial impression persisted to a significant degree. Researchers surmise that once an impression is accepted as fact, it becomes mentally separated from the very information that formed it. Although the information is later discredited, the bogus details are no longer linked to the impression in the observer's mind. "As a result, subsequent challenges to that evidence, and hence to the impression it fostered, will have surprisingly little impact."[13]

Impressive Speeches

I served twelve years on the Board of Education for Holgate Local Schools, presiding for many of those years as president of the board. One of my duties was to present diplomas on graduation day and shake hands with students who successfully graduated from high school. As we waited backstage before the ceremony, I enjoyed joking with the graduating seniors and talking with the student speakers as they rehearsed their lines. The advice I gave them was always the same.

"You know, people will forget what you say within ten minutes after your speech," I told them, "but they will forever remember how they felt about it." Such is the power of impressions, and the long-lasting impact of them.

Nearly Permanent Impressions

Unconscious attitudes, formed implicitly in the mind, function differently than conscious attitudes.[14] Impressions reached by conscious consideration of observed data rely upon the senses to gather information, process details, and determine the impression. An example of a conscious attitude is an impression based on applicant responses to interview questions. The interviewer is pitching questions and scoring each comeback as a hit or an out.

A hiring decision (an example of a conscious attitude) relies upon explicit perceptions which are purposely formed during applicant interviews.[15] Impressions of the applicant quickly become more favorable or less favorable according to how answers match expectations from previous encounters with similar people. Each response creates a conscious decision to affirm or adjust the perception of people who possess the observed traits.

Implicit attitudes (unconscious ones) are often formed without our awareness and are changed only when the memory of similar situations is altered, which takes multiple experiences over a very long time to reset the perception. Without a conscious decision process to judge new acquaintances, unconscious impressions are automatically selected by the brain based on impressions remembered from previous encounters.

It is interesting to note that implicit cues have greater impact than verbal messages in communicating an impression.[16] Additionally, impressions which were formed unconsciously and automatically have been found to be nearly impossible to change even with recent evidence which contradicts previous conclusions. Several consecutive events which refute an impression are required in order to trigger the reconsideration of an implicit perception. Therefore, implicit perceptions almost never change.

The Fugitive

Most people have heard of Dr. Sam Sheppard, who was convicted of killing his wife in 1954 even though there was ample evidence he did not do it. Dr. Sheppard insisted all along that he was innocent and that the real killer escaped after a struggle in the Sheppard home. A popular television show, The Fugitive, carried the plot of the murder case during the 1960's with the character Richard Kimble representing Dr. Sheppard. The case was later revisited during a lengthy appeals process, in which Sheppard was finally exonerated in 1966 when a jury acquitted him.[17] However, many people still believed Dr. Sheppard was guilty.

When The Fugitive was released as a movie in 1993, the case again triggered public interest. The film ended with the capture of the real killer of Richard Kimble's wife. The FBI agent, played by Tommy Lee Jones, acknowledged the doctor's innocence at the end of the film. Ironically, once the popular actor, Harrison Ford, was vindicated as Richard Kimble, the public was persuaded to believe Dr. Sam Sheppard's story.

Resetting Impressions

Multiple interactions provide a series of opportunities to continuously improve our process for forming impressions of others.[18] Even when we have known someone for a long time, impressions are reassessed each time we meet. To a degree "our impressions 'reset' each time we encounter the same person again."[19] Our ability to accurately perceive others requires repeated observations. Much like the effect of product advertising by radio, television, billboards, and social media in which a company brand is formed through a series of repeated impressions, we can all benefit by understanding the long-term impact of continuous data collection in molding the impressions that we determine of others. Likewise, we should be aware of the continuing process in which others modify their impressions of us.

But impressions change slowly. Evaluations which were initially negative have been found to become only slightly more favorable after repeated exposures to positive information.[20] Studies have also found the converse to be true. People who were initially judged positively could behave badly without jeopardizing much of the positive impression that was earlier formed about them. In short, first impressions were nearly permanent and tend to change only after repeated evidence which contradicts the initial impression, resetting the impression in the direction of the newer information.

Flash Forward – The Service Begins at the Chapel

Father David continued his greeting to attendees. "I would like to thank each of you for participating in this memorial service today. We honor the life of a man who has clarified our focus on others around us and one who has inspired us to action as we are reminded to live our lives providing an example for others."

Blessings were extended and people replied with the traditional responses. After a brief prayer from the celebrant, everyone was seated and the lector, one of the brothers from the Chapel, then walked to the pulpit to begin the readings. The friends seated at the front of the Chapel sat back to watch and listen.

At the end of the readings, the lector was replaced at the pulpit by the celebrant, Father David. "I would like to ask Father George to please come forward. He has first-hand knowledge of the long term impact we would like to share with you today and an amazing story."

Impressions can last a very long time!

---

[1] Mary Mitchell, *The First Five Minutes: How to Make a Great First Impression in Any Business Situation* (New York: John Wiley & Sons, Inc. 1998), xvii.

[2] Susan T. Fiske, Monica Lin, and Steven L. Neuberg, "The Continuum Model: Ten Years Later," In *Dual-Process Models in Social Psychology*, eds. Shelly Chaiken and Yaacov Trope (New York: The Guilford Press, 2009), 231-254.

[3] Stephen Porter, Leanne ten Brinke, and Chantal Gustaw, "Dangerous Decisions: The Impact of First Impressions of Trustworthiness on the Evaluation of Legal Evidence and Defendant Culpability," *Psychology, Crime & Law* 16, no. 6 (2010): 479.

[4] Ibid., p. 487.

[5] Stone Phillips, (Anchor), *Dateline NBC,* produced by David Corvo, NBC, aired May 17, 1995, Television.

[6] Ann Demarais and Valerie White, *First Impressions: What You Don't Know About How Others See You* (New York: Bantam Dell, Random House, 2004), 16.

[7] Dennis T. Regan, Ellen Straus, and Russell H. Fazio, "Liking and the Attribution Process," *Journal of Experimental Social Psychology* 10 (1974): 385-397.

[8] John M. Darley and Russell H. Fazio, "Expectancy Confirmation Processes Arising in the Social Interaction Sequence," *American Psychologist* 35 (1980): 876.

[9] "The Power of Purpose," accessed August 24, 2013, http://www.pg.com/en_US/company/purpose_people/index.shtml.

[10] "P & G Corporate Newsroom," accessed August 24, 2013, http://news.pg.com/external_recognition.

[11] Liz McCarthy, (Senior Vice President and Head of Corporate Communications), *"Parallels",* New York Life Insurance, Dec. 22, 2012, Television commercial.

[12] Lee Ross, Mark R. Lepper, and Michael Hubbard, "Perseverance in Self-Perception and Social Perception: Biased Attributional Processes in the Debriefing Paradigm," *Journal of Personality and Social Psychology* 32, no. 5 (1975): 880-892.

[13] Ibid., p. 880.

[14] Robert J. Rydell and others, "Of Two Minds: Forming and Changing Valence Inconsistent Implicit and Explicit Attitudes," *Psychological Science* 17, no. 11 (2006): 954-958.

[15] Ibid

[16] Albert Mehrabian, *Silent Messages: Implicit Communication of Emotions and Attitudes* (Belmont, CA: Wadsworth Publishing, 1981), 77.

[17] Jack DeSario and William D. Mason, *Dr. Sam Sheppard on Trial: The Prosecutors and the Marilyn Sheppard Murder* (Kent, OH: Kent State University Press, 2003), 100.

[18] Vu H. Pham and Lisa Miyake, *Impressive First Impressions: A Guide to the Most Important 30 Seconds (and 30 Years) of Your Career* (Santa Barbara, CA: Praeger, 2010).

[19] Ibid., p. xv.

[20] Allen R. McConnell and others, "Forming Implicit and Explicit Attitudes Toward Individuals: Social Group Association Cues," *Journal of Personality & Social Psychology* 94 (2008): 792-807.

Chapter 6
Positive Impressions

"He who has done his best for his own time has lived for all times."[1] – Johann Christoph Friedrich von Schiller

Father George stepped to the pulpit with his charismatic style and his inviting smile. "I welcome all of you here today, especially the group who made the long journey from the distant region of northwest Ohio," he announced as he looked toward my friends in the front pew. "I have experienced firsthand the drive from Holgate to southern Kentucky, so I know how long it takes. We are glad you can be here to witness our gratitude for the inspiration provided by Dr. Larry Zachrich, or, as I have known him since I first saw the license plate on his car, Dr. Zach. Dr. Zach taught me the lasting impact of our impression on others, which ought to lead us to be on our best behavior. Our positive impressions can benefit those around us."

Flashback – Positive Impressions

Reflecting on positive impressions, I recalled that some of my most favorable impressions are from meetings in Kansas City. I fly into KCI airport, pick up the phone, and dial 26 for the Marriott shuttle. I'm only there four times a year, but the staff remembers me and I am on a first name basis with the shuttle driver, Russ. It is a most entertaining five-minute ride while Russ discusses sports, politics, or the day's headlines during the trip to the hotel.

I have witnessed how he engages all guests. One morning I passed through the hotel lobby on the way to breakfast as he announced the scheduled shuttle was leaving for the airport. A

67

flight crew was waiting in uniform with luggage in tow. As the automatic doors slid open, Russ strode purposefully into the hotel lobby.

"Let's go, Southwest," Russ announced to the airline crew. "It's time to make some money!"

During a recent stay, a waitress named Becky recognized me and warmly asked, "How have you been? You like tomato juice with your coffee, right?" She had remembered my typical request even though it had been several months since I visited.

After a short chat, she left for a minute and cheerfully returned with coffee and juice. I asked, "Are you always so happy or do you just wear that smile for Marriott?"

"I'd say I really am this happy 98% of the time," she replied with a grin, "When you've had really tough times, it teaches you to appreciate what you've got."

The shuttle driver, the restaurant staff, and many other employees at the Kansas City Airport Marriott are truly ambassadors of Marriott. They regularly project a positive impression to guests of their hotel, consistent with one of Marriott's core values – "the belief that people are number one."[2] The hotel chain with 3,700 properties in 74 countries is well represented by hardworking, caring employees who communicate a positive impression.

In his book "The Spirit to Serve", J.W. Marriott, Jr. explains that "truly great companies maintain a set of core values and a core purpose that remain fixed while their business strategies and practices continually adapt to a changing world."[3] There are numerous references to the important roles played by employees, as the key to the company's growth is the realization that success happens through employees. At the heart of Marriott's core values is a focus on people – "Take care of Marriott people and they will take care of Marriott guests."[4] Management is aware that the hotel industry is a team sport and that every organization succeeds through the performance of its team members, projecting a positive impression among their guests.

Creating Positive Images

Because impressions are quick, accurate, and difficult to change, much effort goes into forming a positive impression, even early in life. Parents often admire a traditional fall school photo which appears to capture the image of a kindergarten angel for all of the relatives to enjoy. Those who really know the young lad are fairly certain there is no halo on that head, but horns just below the hair. After a couple of years, his mother bribes the boy into wearing a suit and tie for his first communion day. The image is typically so out of character, as the white trousers and jacket are worlds away from the dirty baseball pants he wore all summer.

Perhaps you have witnessed a high school boy who worked to create a positive image with a prom date, but a staged moment of innocence rarely fools the girl's mother. Nevertheless, we can be certain these facades will be repeated over and over, such is the desire to impress.

We have all observed a friend or colleague in a suit and tie or wearing a new dress. A familiar comment highlights the staged effort as we tell them, "You must be going to a funeral or a job interview." The elaborate apparel is so out of character that observers are quickly aware of the artificially positive appearance. Yet, positive encounters often create long-term memories.

When we recall "the good old days", we are remembering those positive people and events which are quickly recalled from memory by a smell, word, song, or place which reminds us of a happy time. You can surely identify with music, food, or a name which immediately makes you smile. Our beliefs and decisions are sometimes impacted by a favorable impression which was forever imprinted in memory by a genuinely positive experience.

Nothing Runs Like a Deere

"If you're driving a red tractor, you have the wrong tractor!" a close friend once told me. For years I heard people claim they prefer a green tractor over a red one. It always seemed to be a rather silly preference based on color or perhaps the result of better marketing. I thought there might be fewer dealers in the area with red tractors. Then I bought a John Deere lawn tractor.

Customers who drive a John Deere are quick to learn, as the slogan states on their website, that "Nothing Runs Like a Deere."[5] Over multiple years of testing, Consumer Reports National Research Center has verified that John Deere lawn tractors are the best on the market. That rating includes the most recent analysis. Year after year, John Deere has placed three models in the top five tractors manufactured. Most years they produced the number one rated lawn tractor in the United States.[6]

The largest independent nonprofit testing organization in the world has also declared John Deere tractors the most reliable in every year of the survey. John Deere owners have consistently reported the fewest repairs of any manufacturer. The continuing production of high quality tractors, verified through independent testing, leads to a preference for John Deere tractors. Their appeal verifies that businesses enjoying a positive image among customers also profit from a loyal following of repeat business, the result of a positive impression.

Southern Humor

Our friends, Rick and Lisa, invited my wife and I to Charlotte, North Carolina for a weekend. Rick walked us through the renovated downtown and narrated a very interesting tour that was

70

as good, or even better, than a professional tour guide could have delivered. He described the history, identified the architecture, and escorted us into several historic buildings. With his advice, we enjoyed a wonderful lunch in a local hangout.

As we walked down the sidewalk, I noticed brass plates periodically inserted into the cement. I finally stopped to examine a few of them in the middle of the walkway. One plaque seemed particularly intriguing. "This is the spot where Jefferson Davis stood when he learned that Lincoln had been assassinated," I read.

"I know the capital of the Confederacy was in more than one city," I stated and then asked Rick, "Was the capital ever in Charlotte?"

"Oh no," he replied, "the capital was in Birmingham, and then it was moved to Richmond, where it's been ever since." We walked a few more steps while his last several words registered with me and I turned to glance at Rick as he tried his best to hold back a grin.

My sister and her family live in Aiken, South Carolina, so I have traveled to the southeastern part of the country many times. I finally told Rick, "You know, it occurs to me that the key to southern humor is savoring the reaction of Yankees."

I recanted for him a conversation I had enjoyed a few months earlier at the Charlotte Chamber of Commerce. I had met with one of their officials when I planned a student trip to the Carolinas to study the business climate of that region. Attracting thousands of new jobs each year for ten consecutive years, the Charlotte Chamber of Commerce is revered as among the best examples of economic development in the nation.

The employee shared a conversation he had recently conducted. "I once got a call from a fella in Connecticut who had just been appointed to lead the Chamber of Commerce in their county," he explained. "The man told me there were so many praises for Charlotte that he just had to call and ask how we manage to do things so well. I told him when we aren't sure exactly what to do, we call up north and ask y'all for advice. Then we just do the opposite."

He continued his story, "There was dead silence on the other end of the phone, so I finally had to tell the poor guy it was a joke." I have learned to love that southern humor which waits for the reaction of a northerner. The impression left by my friend Rick, and other southern friends, is a combination of humor seasoned with mischief, a most positive impression.

Consumer Satisfaction Over the Years

Johnson & Johnson is the only corporation to be voted one of America's top ten companies for ten consecutive years in two independent reputation surveys. The Reputation Institute, founded in 1997, has conducted an annual survey for Forbes Magazine to measure "seven dimensions of corporate reputation."[7] The most recent results were reported in April of 2013 and included responses by 4,719 consumers, who rated Johnson & Johnson number six in a list of 150 companies. As they have for at least ten straight years, American consumers have demonstrated their loyalty to Johnson & Johnson.

The Harris Poll Reputation Quotient was first administered in the year 2000 and results of the fourteenth annual survey were recently released.[8] Interviews of more than 14,000 people placed Johnson & Johnson in the top five American companies according to perceptions of corporate reputation. In more than half of the surveys over the years, Johnson & Johnson was rated number one in company reputation.

Consumers have consistently demonstrated their loyalty and confidence in the company's responsibility to customers, employees, management, community and stockholders.

Perceptions of the company may have been formed years earlier, but customer opinions have been frequently reinforced by experiences with quality products which led them to confirm that their faith in Johnson & Johnson is a genuinely positive impression.

Lasting Positive and Negative Memories

Undoubtedly, people have planted impressions in our memories, positive and negative, during the course of their lives. Some of our best memories are moments in which someone left a favorable imprint whether they realize it or not. When we encounter a similar scene later in life, their positive memory quickly returns to the front of our awareness.

Likewise, there have been negative experiences, perhaps tragedies, that follow us continuously just below the surface of our consciousness. On any given day, a simple event such as a calendar date, a word, a song, or even a smell can conjure up a vivid image that just can't be shaken loose as it comes rushing back to us. However, in most cases we are able to enjoy positive aspects of memories while suppressing the negative effects.

Each of us has communicated positive and negative images to others, who perceived us as either a favorable or an uncomplimentary memory. None of us is entirely good or bad. We are each a combination of behaviors which have created positive and negative impressions.

A Fine Line Between Positive and Negative Impressions

My grandson's final baseball game last summer was a memorable event for me. Actually, it was a great game for him as well. Breyer caught a line drive which was hit to right-center field for the third out of the inning with runners on base, a memory he can carry with him into next season. I was very pleased with that play, but the impression I took away was the comment of two fans I overheard as they arrived midway through the game.

As a frowning man dragged his lawn chair to the third base side of the field, I heard him mutter, "I wonder how many runs we are behind by now!"

A moment later, a fourth grader stopped his bicycle in front of me and asked, "Which run is that guy we are about to score?" as he pointed to our player standing on third base.

When they had continued past me, I reflected on their comments. They were both asking the same question, "What is the score?" However, one was negative and the other was positive. The first was cynical, while the second was optimistic.

I had previously noticed the difference between hosts in a local restaurant. When a couple walked in the door, one greeter asked, "Are there only two of you?" The other host later greeted a couple by asking, "Will there be two of you joining us for dinner tonight?" I thought to myself that the wording was much more respectful toward the second group. However, the essential question was the same for both. The main point was to determine how many seats were needed for the people in their party.

If there is one thing I have learned in a 40-year career, it is that "how" you do things is often more important than "what" you do. People really do develop an impression which is positive or negative based upon how we behave.

The First Impression As A Lasting Impression

Each of us routinely records a mental first impression when encountering a stranger. We quickly interpret that first impression based on our only observation. If new acquaintances are never seen again, people leave our lives as quickly as they entered. For those one-time encounters, the first impression also becomes a lasting impression of our only chance to observe.

Management consultant, Renee Evenson, believes "every time you are in a situation for the first time, you will be making a first impression on someone."[9] That realization leads us to consider our behavior when meeting others and to second guess whether we might have projected the kind of image we desire, whether we have communicated the impression we believe to be genuine, because it is likely to be remembered for a long time.

Reflection on Multiple Kindnesses

Father George resumed his presentation to those assembled for the memorial service at the Chapel. "Dr. Zach has written extensively on lasting impressions such as the National Park Service employee who inspired his book," he explained. "I have never been accused of being a mathematician, but I have done some quick calculations on the influence of lasting impressions. If the Park Service employee directly inspired one person each week, then he has touched at least 600 people since 2004. If each of them influenced a single person each month over all those years, there are more than 40,000 people inspired. If individuals acted charitably twice each year, then that means 80,000 acts of kindness have been performed. It is Dr. Zach who communicated that example and it is through him that others have been motivated by lasting impressions."

"We seldom realize our influence on others," Father George continued. "Although life presents many twists and turns, a positive impression ultimately inspires a favorable outcome. This story leads to an interesting final positive impression."

Positive impressions can have a powerful impact on others!

[1] Johann Christoph Friedrich von Schiller (translated by M. Verkruzen), *Wallenstein's Lager* (Hamburg: The Author, 1899), 11.

[2] J. Willard Marriott and Kathi A. Brown, *The Spirit to Serve: Marriott's Way* (New York, NY: Harper Collins, 1997), xii.

[3] Ibid., p. xii.

[4] Ibid., p. xiii.

[5] "Residential" accessed August 21, 2013, ttp://www.deere.com/wps/dcom/en_US/industry/residential/residential.page?

[6] "Lawn Tractors," *Consumer Reports Buying Guide* 77, no. 13 (2013): 79-81.

[7] Jacquelyn Smith, "America's Most Reputable Companies", last modified April 24,2013,http://www.forbes.com/sites/jacquelynsmith/2013/04/24/americas-most-reputable-companies-/?utm_source=huffingtonpost.com&utm_medium=partner&utm_campaign=most+reputable+companies&partner=huffpo.

[8] Harris Interactive, "The Harris Poll Reputation Quotient", accessed July 9, 2013, http://www.harrisinteractive.com/vault/2013%20RQ%20Summary%20Report%20FINAL.pdf.

[9] Renee Evenson, "Making a Great First Impression," *Techniques: Connecting Education & Careers* 82, no. 5 (2007): 17.

Chapter 7
Negative Impressions

"Make a poor first impression, and that may very well be the last impression you have the opportunity to make."[1] – Renee Evenson

"It would benefit each of us to reflect on whether we have helped those in need," Father George continued to share advice at the Chapel. "Dr. Zach's story has identified an inspirational event which impacted his life and which inspires all of us to reflect on our own lives. We can all strive to improve. It is not that we are bad people, we are not intentionally negative, but we could sometimes do better. The good news is, if we are not quite satisfied with our impression thus far, we can work to improve."

Flashback – Negative Impressions

As I reflected on Father George's comments, I recalled examples of impressions which could stand a little improving, some which included me. When I was 18 years old, I was out drinking one night with my friend, Kirk. After too many hours in the bar, and a few too many beers, we headed for home. I was either driving fast, not paying attention, talking too much, or some combination of reasons. I suddenly saw we were nearing the highway with too little time to slow down for the stop sign. There were corn fields on each side of us, so we could not see if there was traffic on the highway. We had no choice but to ride it out.

I warned Kirk, "We can't stop, so hang on!"

I cringed as we drove right through the stop sign, but we crossed the highway with no traffic in sight. As we came to a stop, we both realized how lucky we had been. We could just as easily have caused a tragic accident with long-term consequences. Even though that event was forty years ago, we have both learned to value a designated driver when we decide to enjoy a few drinks.

I recently retold that story to my friend, Pastor Marcis, and explained to him that it is one of those negative experiences in life where we were just lucky. He agreed, but also identified that we all need to be aware of defining moments in life.

As Pastor Marcis explained, "We all stumble at times with wrong choices. The important part is whether we learn from our mistakes. We all benefit from our errors if they become a turning point which improves our behavior."

Selfish Behavior

Sometimes it isn't a foul word or a dastardly deed which projects a negative impression. The perception of an event which is labeled negative may be determined by the eye of the beholder.

While I was at the Myrtle Beach airport waiting for my flight to Detroit, I observed the formation of a negative impression. Thirty people waited to board a plane for Atlanta in a very slow line, many without patience. The last woman in the long procession had a dark tan, thin build, and expensive dress. She must have decided that the wait was too long, so she confidently stepped out of line and pulled her bag-on-wheels past all of the other waiting passengers, walking with a strut usually reserved for a Victoria Secret model wearing the latest fashion on the runway. Twelve men stared all the way, six of them with chin dropped and mouth wide open, two suffering a quick elbow in the gut from a frowning wife as the woman neared the gate attendant. With three men motioning for her to step into the line, she easily chose a spot at the front and handed over her boarding pass.

As the woman disappeared into the jet bridge, the men regained consciousness. I noticed three females at the back of the line talking in loud tones with frowns on their faces, pointing toward what they had just witnessed. When the line had dwindled and it was finally their turn to board, the women stopped long enough to scold the gate attendant before entering the jet bridge. While I suspect a dozen men will not soon forget the impression they witnessed in Myrtle Beach, the passenger who "butted" in line had created a negative impression on others.

Some Impressions Are Not Favorable

Since impressions are so fast, accurate, and stubborn, you really don't want to leave a negative image. Renee Evenson, a management consultant for several companies in employee hiring processes, warns applicants of the consequences of a negative first impression.[2] With only a few seconds to impress, you can't waste a moment. Researchers have found that judgments within a few seconds can be as accurate as longer observations.[3] The perception which leads to a negative impression is just as fast and seemingly accurate as a positive first impression.

My brain has stored a special impression of people who walk with a hop in their step. I'm sure you have seen them, as the heel of the foot quickly rises with each step as if they need to become an inch taller. I have filed that trait in a folder labeled "smart aleck." Before I consciously consider my reaction, a new acquaintance walking with that hop is already labeled negatively. It is difficult for people with that walk to achieve a positive impression in my mind.

You might also recall people and events in your own life which imprinted a negative impression on you. The image is then committed to memory, from which it is quickly recalled when making decisions. Later in life those negative feelings jump to the front of our minds and vividly steer our decisions, even if we don't remember how they were formed.

The New Coke Alienated Customers

"Depending on who you ask, it was one of the greatest marketing blunders in history (as most would say) or an unlikely stroke of corporate genius (as a diehard few still maintain)."[4] On April 23, 1985, the Coca-Cola Company told the world it was dropping its original formula in favor of a sweeter version that more closely resembled its competitors. The company had no idea the decision would alienate diehard Coke fans.

Concern for an increasing market share at Pepsi, and unfavorable taste test results, had led to development of a sweeter recipe. The company had completely overlooked the history of customer loyalty, thinking a new taste was more important.

After a barrage of complaints, the company retracted their decision three months later, announcing the return of the original formula now called "Coca-Cola Classic". Sales for the original Coca-Cola surged, restoring it as the dominant leader in the competitive soda market. In fact, sales increased so much due to the special attention that their market share ultimately grew. The company later tried to resurrect the replacement drink as "Coke II", but the despised impostor quickly faded into oblivion until it was mostly forgotten. Once consumers have been alienated, the negative impression is firmly planted in their minds, and decision making behavior typically follows the lead of their impression.

Impact of Negative Impressions

Studies suggest that negative impressions, such as people labeled "threatening", are processed even faster than positive impressions.[5] "It is conceivable that our visual system has evolved to detect face information pertaining to threat evaluations at a lower threshold, and thus at a faster rate, on the basis of information that is available first."[6] We have developed visual processes to quickly form impressions as a defense mechanism when we sense danger.

Political impressions drawn from negative information are convincing and long lasting, as most election campaigns indicate that attack advertising can be more effective than positive marketing strategies.[7] Negative events often prove more influential than positive statements in the ability to form impressions.[8] Therefore, negative conclusions are not only more quickly formed in the minds of perceivers, but they are more permanently etched in memory.

A Playboy Politician

When I watched the televised Democratic National Convention in 2012, I was reminded once again that Bill Clinton can deliver a very good speech. The imagery was captivating and his style is still convincing. The familiar appearance of Bill Clinton, the confident sound of his voice, and his friendly style mentally drew me back to a time of economic prosperity and a federal budget surplus. His message outshined all of the other speakers at the convention.

However, I cannot forget a mental image of Bill Clinton with Monica Lewinski and a tell-tale stain on her blue dress. On August 17, 1998 the DNA tests performed by the FBI concluded that "based on the results of these seven genetic loci, specimen K39 (CLINTON) is the source of the DNA obtained from specimen Q3243-1, to a reasonable degree of scientific certainty."[9] People sometimes create a negative impression which will not go away, regardless how badly they might wish it would.

The Doping News Just Wouldn't Go Away

For years all of America had bristled at any inference that Lance Armstrong might have used performance enhancing drugs.

After all, he had beaten cancer with the same determination that led him to defeat every other cyclist in the world. However, the accusations just wouldn't go away and the questions began to mount. Eventually every sponsor retracted their support of Lance Armstrong by ending endorsement contracts.

Nike was the major sponsor to withdraw by explaining, "Due to the seemingly insurmountable evidence that Lance Armstrong participated in doping and misled Nike for more than a decade, it is with great sadness that we have terminated our contract with him. Nike does not condone the use of illegal performance enhancing drugs in any manner."[10]

Although nobody wanted to believe it, the loyal support eventually caved in to the reality of a negative impression. Lance Armstrong finally confessed to using performance-enhancing drugs in front of a television audience on January 17, 2013.[11] Although many viewers failed to see remorse, at least the issue of doping was clarified once and for all. Unfortunately for Lance Armstrong, the lasting impression will continue to be negative.

What Is the Real Focus?

As I recently sat in a restaurant, I overheard two women discussing the recent Sunday service at their church. "I came back to the area after being away for a few years and discovered a realization about the church service here," one of them stated. "The organ is elaborate and the organist did a fine job. He even directed the choir, which sang beautifully. However, the service seemed to take a back seat to the music. It was actually more of a concert than a service."

"I am more accustomed to a focus on how we can improve our lives to get to heaven, but I didn't hear any of that," she continued. "At the end of the service a couple more anthems were sung and people actually applauded the organist and choir. It all seemed to distract from the real purpose of church. I got the impression that many people approved, as if they would rather be entertained. I might be looking for a different church, because this one is not serious."

There Is No "I" in Team

A former president of the College liked to remind employees that "'there is no 'I' in the word 'team'." The leader was quick to thank others and to compliment them on their individual achievements which contributed toward the success of the whole organization. He was keenly aware that an accomplishment for one was a victory for all. The president went out of his way to get to know each employee on campus and to give them credit for successes. At the time he retired, we were the fastest growing college in the state of Ohio for five consecutive years.

Unfortunately, his replacement had no interest in teamwork and preferred to take credit for every success on campus. I once suggested to her that one of our coworkers was a classic two-year college success story. She quickly informed me that we did not need to recognize his accomplishments.

"I am the success story here," the new president replied. "I will be the example on this campus."

Instead of recognition or appreciation, employees learned to expect retribution. Soon there was little innovation and certainly no risk taking. Everyone seemed to hunker down in a "bunker mentality", most of them constantly vigilant for her next critique. The standard operating procedure became looking over one's shoulder. Productivity quickly declined, along with the student enrollment. The new president had quickly dismantled the successful organization that she inherited, while she stroked her ego and padded her personal resume. Long after she had left the institution, her name continued to elicit a negative impression.

Opportunities for Improvement

Father George explained to the audience at the Chapel, "While we may feel guilty when our inward reflection discovers negative impressions, we should appreciate the reality that we can improve. We have opportunities to turn our negative impressions into more positive influences. Dr. Zach taught me the phrase "Opportunities for Improvement". We can learn from others, as the story I share today. One man's final impression inspires us to improve."

We can learn from negative impressions!

---

[1] Renee Evenson, "Making a Great First Impression," *Techniques: Connecting Education & Careers* 82, no. 5 (2007): 14-17.

[2] Ibid.

[3] Nalini Ambady and Robert R. Rosenthal, "Thin Slices of Expressive Behavior As Predictors of Interpersonal Consequences: A Meta-Analysis," *Psychological Bulletin* 111, no. 2 (1992): 256.

[4] "Down the Sink: Coke*"* accessed July 3, 2013, http://www.time.com/time/specials/packages/article/0,28804,1913612_1913610_1913608,00.html.

[5] Moshe Bar, Maital Neta, and Heather Linz, "Very First Impressions," *Emotion* 6, no. 2 (2006): 269-278.

[6] Ibid., p. 276.

[7] Michael D. Cobb, and James H. Kuklinski, "Changing Minds: Political Arguments and Political Persuasion," *American Journal of Political Science* 41, no. 1 (1997): 88-121.

[8] Paul Slovic, "Perceived Risk, Trust, and Democracy," *Risk Analysis* 13 (1993): 675-682.

[9] "Report of Examination," *Federal Bureau of Investigation* (1998): (29D-O1C-LR-35063).

[10] "Nike Statement on Lance Armstrong," accessed Oct. 17, 2012, http://www.nikeinc.com/news/nike-statement-on-lance-armstrong.

[11] Oprah Winfrey, "Oprah and Lance Armstrong: The Worldwide Exclusive, Part 1," *Oprah's Next Chapter*, Oprah Winfrey Network, aired Jan. 17, 2013, Television.

Chapter 8
False Impressions

Deception has existed since "the serpent in the Garden of Eden."[1]
– C. Bond and B. DePaulo

As the group sat in the front row at the Chapel, Alice commented to Sandy, "I thought that sharing the lasting impression example was Larry's reason to write his book. However, I had missed the main point of the story, his true motivation. As he got further into his writing, Larry became more focused on persuading others that each of us has a lesson to teach. Each of us has a valuable inspiration that is worthwhile to pass on to benefit others, that each of us can determine our legacy."

We are each capable of interpreting a wrong impression from time to time. The problem with some of those perceptions is that they might lead our decisions astray. The first impressions are not very useful, then, when our perceptions of people are faulty.

Flashback – Experiencing False Impressions

You might recall times when your first impression was wrong. Perhaps there were people who imprinted an immediate impression on you which later proved to be false. When a product or service disappoints, we feel tricked by the seller. If a person is not genuine, we feel betrayed. The image committed to memory, and applied to the decision making process, had been a mistake. Impressions which were quick, accurate, and long lasting are not worthwhile if the basis of the perception is not genuine. I can recall times that I have been deceived by a false impression.

It Takes a Thief

My colleague, Von, and I had been traveling on a business trip when we witnessed an entertaining impression. Our connection through Detroit airport included a two-hour layover, so I knew there would be a long wait. As we stepped off the first plane, I suggested that we stop at a bar in the terminal for a sandwich and a Coke. My Detroit Tigers were playing baseball on the television and that seemed like a pleasant way to pass the time.

When we entered, a different type of entertainment presented itself. A young woman began yelling that she was robbed. Our nearby table provided a perfect view. I remember feeling like it was live theater and we had the best seats in the house.

"Someone stole a thousand dollars from my purse and it was the bartender!" she shouted. "Who's going to do something?"

Without speaking the bartender walked to the phone and pushed some buttons. He had quickly assessed the situation and knew how to deal with it. However, the woman wasn't going to quit and the manager arrived just as she erupted again.

"What are you going to do about this?" she screamed, as she pointed a finger in the boss's face. "I want my money back."

Just then two police officers arrived on bicycles at the entrance to the bar. Their yellow spandex uniforms and multi-colored helmets added to the humor of the scene. They quickly took charge, as they each grabbed one of the woman's wrists.

"I'm not leaving without my money!" the woman shouted.

"You're not leaving without paying your bar tab!" the manager interjected.

Everyone froze in place for a long moment. Even the police weren't certain how to resolve the woman's debt. Finally, a man seated at the bar said, "I'll pay her bill." The manager quickly presented a slip of paper and, as the bar patron opened his wallet, the police officers dragged the woman out the door. Before the billfold returned to his pocket, the gentleman was confronted by a bald-headed man who had slowly walked toward the bar with a wide grin on his face. I had seen the man enjoying the live theater from across the room and he now decided to become involved.

"So, do you feel taken yet?" the antagonist asked the man who had paid the woman's bar tab. "You know this was all a scam, don't you?" There was no reply. "She planned this all along and you just became the patsy who got stuck with the bill." He returned to his seat, still grinning from ear to ear.

I was lamenting the end of the show and checked the score of the baseball game, which had continued without anyone watching. As I picked up my half-eaten sandwich, the relative calm was interrupted by the same shrill voice.

"I still want my thousand dollars!" The woman screamed as she stomped back into the bar. The bartender reached for the phone once more and I sat up in my chair, again happy to be positioned at the closest table to the action. I could see a wide grin on the bald man across the room, as he also sensed the opportunity for more comedy. When his eyes met mine, he gave me the thumbs up sign, indicating his approval of the live theater.

"The rest of you had better hold onto your money because there's a thief working here!" she shouted, throwing her suitcase as she yelled. The bag sailed through the air, ricocheted off the floor, and the extended handle hit Von in the back as he sat opposite me. He popped into the air as if he had been launched out of his chair and quickly turned toward the lady.

"I believe it's time for you to leave," Von told the woman.

"Is that so?" she replied with one hand on her hip and the other pointing a finger in Von's face. "Well I believe that you are an asshole!"

I could hardly keep from laughing out loud and the bald man across the room had given up maintaining his composure, as he was laughing face down, slapping the table with his palm. Just as quickly as she had returned, the woman was suddenly grabbed by both arms and dragged out the door by the same two police officers. "She won't be coming back this time," one policeman stated as they escorted the woman out the door.

The real thief was the woman with the ruse of stolen money. She might have scammed the bar patron into paying her tab, but she hadn't fooled anyone with her claim of theft. My friend, Von, and I have discussed the ability to discern truthfulness from lies. He describes the skill as his "BS Meter", which is activated whenever he hears a less than credible message.

The woman's lasting impression verified my belief in the live theater which is playing constantly around us. While I was disappointed her show had ended, I am convinced there is a continuous production of the human experience if we only take the time to notice. We are all spectators and, whether we volunteer or not, some of us become actors, occasionally dragged onto the stage of life. We sometimes participate in the impressions being formed around us, and we must be leery of false impressions.

Problematic Impressions

We are vulnerable to relying on false impressions because there are several reasons an individual may not project a realistic image. First, perceivers can be misled because the observer will be unaware if the impression they perceive is not representative of the person's normal behavior.[2] It is possible for a student to perform poorly on a test due to illness, just as a person may be viewed in apparel which is not typically worn or someone may be observed when suffering physical pain. While the image being projected is not characteristic, an observer is unaware that a perception at that time will be erroneous.

Secondly, the subject of an observation may be so cunning that it is possible for him to manipulate a perception. The person who is the focus of review often recognizes expectations of the observer, and then adapts responses accordingly. "The target, in effect, becomes a perceiver", learning to play the interviewer according to his own intentions.[3] At that point, the behavior of the individual being observed is staged, leading to a false impression.

Third, it is possible that the perceiver has predetermined expectancies of a subject due to stereotypes regarding personal traits. Many decisions we make in life depend on perceptions formed during previous events. A history with those past outcomes leads us to create mental shortcuts for later decision making as judgmental heuristics or "rules of thumb". When we rely on a mental rule of thumb for a new impression, it creates a short cut for us to quickly reach a decision without conscious thought. Unfortunately, research has identified that the use of judgmental heuristics is associated with errors and biases.[4]

Fourth, there are times when the judgment of a subject is influenced by the environment. An observer may assume that a person is viewed in normal context, when the surroundings may not be at all typical of the subject's environment. Therefore, the physical setting of an observation may lead to an impression which is perceived out of context.

Deceptive Hiring Credentials

The board of directors at Yahoo hired the former president of eBay subsidiary, PayPal, to lead the corporation at a challenging time. Scott Thompson had years of experience in management and technology positions along with significant awards. In January of 2012 he seemed to have just the right background and resume to lead a high-tech company. However, five months later the resume didn't appear quite as perfect. The bio with a bachelor's degree in computer science from Stonehill College became a focus of concern when it was discovered that the degree program did not exist at the college until four years after Thompson's graduation.

The Chief Executive Officer of Yahoo resigned from his leadership position in May of 2012 when it was discovered he had a false college degree in his biography. The headline read, "Thompson has come under fire for lying about his academic degrees."[5] The CEO and Yahoo claimed the bachelor's degree in computer science was an accidental error when it was printed in the biography. However, others are not so sure there was an accident in his resume. "It is so clear-cut whether one has a degree or not that it is a deliberate lie and the only reason to do it is to misrepresent yourself," said Janice Bellace, professor of business ethics at the Wharton School, University of Pennsylvania.[6]

The effect of false information is so devastating that current managers and students of business should take note of the ramifications of misrepresentation on one's career. When personal information is found to be false, the impression is immediate, negative, and impossible to change. In most cases, a perception of deception will trump a successful employment record.

The Failure of Our Impressions

Without an effective warning of potential deceit, we are often oblivious to false impressions. A review of deception research analyzed 206 studies performed prior to 2006, including more than 24,000 observers who judged almost 7,000 messages received from over 4,000 senders as new acquaintances.[7] The overall average rate of correct classification in judgments of lies and truth was 53.98%, barely above a 50% random chance. Therefore, people are hardly better than the flip of a coin, fifty – fifty, in their ability to determine the presence of deception when observing first impressions of dishonest individuals.

A recent study compared skills of experienced human resource professionals with those of amateur observers. Recruiters averaged six years of experience and eighteen months of recruitment training, while amateurs had zero experience or training. Experienced recruiters were confident they could detect lies in job applicants, but doubted the ability of inexperienced students.[8] However, the difference between the groups was slight and even professionals were often fooled. People cannot readily detect deception and applicants routinely employ strategies to embellish impressions, which is sometimes referred to as "impression management". It was determined that both amateurs and professional interviewers were similarly vulnerable to impression management.[9] Therefore, experienced deceivers in all walks of life have been found to be quite believable when manipulating their impression on observers.

A Good Neighbor?

Altemio Sanchez and his family lived in a quiet Buffalo neighborhood for almost thirty years, playing golf and working at the local factory. He was a hard worker at the same local job for twenty-three years. Sanchez hosted a neighborhood cookout each summer and frequently coached basketball teams and softball teams, including children of friends and neighbors. He was a meticulous gardener and shared vegetables with everyone in the subdivision. Neighbors viewed Altemio as friendly and helpful to all, a model citizen as far as his neighbors knew.

However, Sanchez was convicted of committing three murders and eight rapes over 23 years.[10] The judge at his trial ordered him to serve a sentence of seventy-five years to life in prison. His DNA has since been linked to many more sexual assaults in the Buffalo area. A neighbor of 28 years, Jerry Donohue, stated "the scary part is, he's the nicest person you'd

91

ever want to meet."[11] The "Bike Path Rapist" had fooled everyone by his deceptive impression.

False Impressions Due to Planned Deception

While many errors in developing first impressions have been identified as flaws in the observation process, false perceptions are often caused by outright deceit. Researchers have found it is not uncommon for deception to bias conclusions of observers.[12] When deceit is purposely employed, all bets are off regarding accuracy. Unfortunately, manipulated impressions can be just as fast as those which are genuine and might last a long time even though they are false because the perceiver is caught off guard by the deception.

Most of us tend to be trusting and believe truthfulness to be the norm, so the majority of people are easily fooled. "They accept most statements at face value, rarely inquiring into the authenticity of what they hear."[13] However, our faith in humankind is often betrayed by deceivers with an opposite view that scamming people is normal.

Medicinal Yogurt?

For two years Dannon had been promoting Activia and DanActive yogurt as "proven to regulate digestion and boost immune systems".[14] However, in 2010 the Federal Trade Commission investigation found there was no basis for the claims. The company later agreed to settle a deceptive advertising lawsuit initiated by the FTC and the attorneys general of thirty-nine states. Terms of the settlement included a payment of $21 million to the states and an agreement to end claims which overstate the health benefits of their products.

Jon Leibowitz, chairman of the Federal Trade Commission, explained, "Consumers want, and are entitled to, accurate information when it comes to their health. Companies like

Dannon shouldn't exaggerate the strength of scientific support for their products."[15] Unfortunately, the deception by sellers is a common scenario. However, it is also typical for customers to walk away from a company that deceives them. It would be far easier to maintain the public trust with accurate statements than to regain the confidence of customers who have been alienated.

The Rise of Deception

Deception is simply the normal state of interaction for those who practice deceit. "To the liar, there is nothing exceptional about lying."[16] Individuals often alter their appearance to change their identity or to shape others' impressions of them. Some simply rearrange the facts.

Every used car salesman seems to have "the best deal" on his car lot and a smooth talking salesman can often overcome reservations on the part of hesitant buyers. A product with a "money back guarantee" is often irresistible, but elusive when we attempt to enforce the promise. We often place confidence in first impressions which have been manipulated. Unfortunately, "if we don't have time for second or third impressions, then that can lead to wrong decisions."[17]

Valid perceptions can be easily hindered by experienced deceivers, as the ability to accurately read facial expressions is limited to those subjects whose appearance is genuine.[18] Unfortunately for observers, it is impossible to know if you are judging an honest person or a deceitful individual during a single observation. Those who rely on deception are usually able to draw upon a history of tricks and illusions which effectively hide their dishonesty.

"Putting your best foot forward" has been a popular strategy for years, with a focus on projecting a positive appearance. However, the recent emphasis is on "creating a favorable impression." The former strategy highlighted your own traits, while the latter has no remorse if you simply "make it up as you go." Whenever a person behaves in the presence of others, there is usually a reason for him to charm them to convey an impression which is in his best interest.[19] Although we are naturally skeptical of others, we are still disappointed when fooled.

Holiday Cheer?

I was never one of those serious "Black Friday" shoppers. However, one year I agreed to tag along with Alice to the mall on the day after Thanksgiving. I only lasted a couple of hours, but others seemed to run a dawn to dusk marathon of "shop 'til you drop." Even the Santa Claus had put in a long day, as evidenced by his conversation with the store employee who accompanied him at the closing of his workshop.

As he quickly departed from the temporary North Pole, I overheard him complaining, "That's enough of those damn kids. I need a cold beer!"

I thought to myself, "That's not exactly the 'Miracle on 34th Street' over there." But then, I guess each of us is still a work in process, hoping to improve.

Deception Studies

A review of job applicants who embellished traits in interviews has led authors to recommend structuring employment interviews with a strategy to combat impression manipulation.[20] Employers have become increasingly wary of deceptive applicants, just as the general public has become leery of false advertising.

Job applicants have also been found to fake their work histories.[21] "The art of acting is the art of impression management."[22] Subjects have learned to create positive traits to project favorable impressions during hiring processes. "To the extent that applicants try to appear in the best light possible and use different impression management strategies to do so, deception detection becomes an important topic in personnel selection."[23]

"The employment interview is a prime place for candidates to manage impressions due to its interpersonal nature, ambiguity, short duration, and high stakes."[24] A new study from CareerBuilder.com cautions job seekers about the references they cite when applying to companies. "Three-in-five employers (62 percent) said that when they contacted a reference listed on an application, the reference didn't have good things to say about the candidate."[25] In 29% of cases, employers reported that they have caught a fake reference on a candidate's application.

Justice Is Blind

The justice system in the United States relies heavily upon accuracy in forming first impressions of witnesses. It is expected that jury members will distinguish truth from falsehood and separate guilt from innocence. While it is generally believed that people can determine credibility, a recent study concluded that errors in deception detection occur 45% of the time.[26]

Although judges and law enforcement officials are confident in their ability to reach decisions, data has shown that they are no more effective than laypersons, and no better than random chance at detecting deception in the credibility of subjects.[27] In some experiments trained police officers were less accurate than amateurs. In one study participants were asked to evaluate faces of criminals (America's Most Wanted subjects) and those of humanitarian award winners (such as the Nobel Peace Prize).[28] Viewers erred in judgments half the time, as trustworthiness is difficult to assess in those who are skilled in deception.

Laypeople as well as law enforcement professionals believe liars exhibit signs of deception such as avoiding eye contact.

However, studies have shown liars to focus more deliberate eye contact than truthful people.[29] Deceivers need to monitor the effect of false claims on others, so they tend to look intently at their victims. Therefore, observers often misjudge the trustworthiness of strangers by misinterpreting the effect of eye contact in first impressions.

Studies have shown that professional "lie catchers" were no more effective than amateur citizens with a success rate of only 56% accuracy compared with the 54% accuracy rate of amateurs.[30] Ironically, "criminals were one of the most accurate groups in detecting deception" when catching people who were lying.[31]

A Smooth Talker

An intelligent, well dressed law school student successfully won over women with his handsome appearance and charismatic style. He seemed to charm them at will, motivating them to accompany him. What they surely didn't know were his motives of kidnapping, assault, and murder. The positive first impression that gained their trust was certainly not accurate, as Ted Bundy captured and killed more than thirty women. He impressed dozens of females and then abused their trust.

Ann Rule recalls nothing disturbing in Ted Bundy's personality while she was a coworker, describing him as a kind and empathetic person.[32] She remembers that "he became an honor student, and was well-regarded by his professors."[33] As his enlightened biographer, Ann Rule later described his evil as "a sadistic sociopath who took pleasure from another human's pain and the control he had over his victims, to the point of death, and even after."[34] Years after his execution by electric chair in Florida, authorities still speculate on the number of women he killed. The extent of his deception and his ability to lure women with false impressions are still mysterious.

Consequences of Deception

"The interactional problem with first impressions is not that we form them, but that they can be incorrect."[35] "Errors can be consequential because untrustworthy salespeople, executives, politicians, and con artists are constantly trying to gain our trust" when they do not deserve it.[36]

A clever charlatan can sometimes ruin our ability to arrive at accurate, fast impressions. "Only when an individual actively tries to portray deceptive thoughts and feelings does our accuracy falter."[37] "Unfortunately for the perceiver, it appears that skills in detecting deception lag behind skills in perpetrating deception."[38] "Perhaps the real tragedy of the behavioral consequences of first impressions is that we rarely discover when our impressions have led us awry" until it is too late.[39]

The process of successfully judging individuals requires skepticism and advanced knowledge regarding the traits of those who employ deception. Effective deceivers are usually expressive, socially tactful, and possess high levels of cognitive ability.[40] In other words, they are smooth talkers, mingle well with others, and are intelligent. Their skills make them successful manipulators, as they are usually believable in their efforts to deceive.

Deceptive impressions work best in short bursts of limited interactions. Behaving in ways which are inconsistent with one's true personality requires great psychological effort.[41] Therefore, if pressed with questions, viewed in repeated observations, or observed during lengthy interviews, manipulators are less effective.[42] However, experienced deceivers are well aware of their limitations and they will create elaborate reasons to limit the number of observations, as well as the longevity of interactions, to protect their deception. They function much like magicians who rely upon distractions and quick movements to protect themselves from revealing real intentions and their true nature. If we are

97

vigilant, we can detect deception and identify a genuine impression after multiple encounters in which to acquire more data.

Self-Inflicted Judgment Problems

The ability to arrive at accurate first impressions is sometimes compromised by our eagerness to believe others. In one study observers were told truths and lies by friends they had known for hardly six months. Although they had not known the subjects for very long, and were specifically told to watch for cues of honesty and evidence of deceit when stories were told to them, perceivers could not manage to separate truth from fiction.[43] Even a short-term friendship had created a familiarity bias. At times we might sabotage ourselves in our inability to recognize the truth about others due to an assumed connection with them.

Several reasons cause us to fail in our perceptions. First, we possess an "optimism bias." "This is our tendency to overestimate the likelihood that good things will happen to us and underestimate the potential for unpleasant events."[44]

Secondly, studies have revealed that impression judgments are unduly influenced by extreme attributes of people.[45] We tend to overreact against subjects whose traits and behaviors appear negative and those who appear extremely different from our views.

Third, we are prone to a "confirmation bias." Any information which appears to confirm our belief is accepted at face value and becomes evidence to corroborate the first opinion. It appears we possess a "need to be right."

Fourth, we are "subconsciously stubborn" in our insistence to support an initial impression. According to Pat Huddleston, former enforcement officer for the Securities and Exchange Commission, "when we get a fact that doesn't quite fit in the puzzle, we force it in."[46] This often leads us to be naïve in our trusting attitude when we should have been suspicious.

Prepare for an Unexpected Impression

As I listened to Father George, it occurred to me that the significant impression is often different from the perception that first meets the eye. For example, there is a false impression about the effect of charity which is seldom realized by the donor. While it appears recipients of generosity are the ones who benefit, those who help them are the ones truly blessed by their action. In the end, the donor has more to gain by the opportunity to be generous than those who receive a donation, as it truly is better to give than to receive. Interestingly, those who receive often later become donors to others, thus perpetuating the generosity.

Father George continued, "We sometimes perceive a false impression until the true meaning of an event is revealed. You are about to learn an amazing impression, an outcome of Dr. Zach's story, and it may be a completely different impression than you expected."

We must be wary of false impressions!

---

[1] Charles F. Bond and Bella M. DePaulo, "Accuracy of Deception Judgments," *Personality and Social Psychology Review* 10, no. 3 (2006): 214.

[2] John M. Darley and Russell H. Fazio, "Expectancy Confirmation Processes Arising in the Social Interaction Sequence," *American Psychologist* 35, no. 10 (1980): 867-881.

[3] Ibid., p. 871.

[4] Daniel Kahneman and Amos Tversky, "Causal Schemas in Judgments Under Uncertainty," in *Judgment under uncertainty: Heuristics and biases,* eds. Daniel Kahneman and Amos Tversky, (Cambridge, UK: Cambridge University Press, 1982), 117.

[5] Melinda Blackman, "What Yahoo CEO's False Bio Tells Us About Resume Fraud," last modified May 12, 2012, http://www.cnn.com/2012/05/12/opinion/blackman-resume-fraud/index.html.

[6] Nick Turner and Dina Bass, "Yahoo Investor Steps Up Pressure to Have CEO Fired," last modified May 5, 2012, http://www.businessweek.com/news/2012-05-05/yahoo-board-to-review-ceo-credentials-after-criticism#p1.

[7] Charles F. Bond and Bella M. DePaulo, "Accuracy of Deception Judgments," *Personality and Social Psychology Review* 10, no. 3 (2006): 214-234.

[8] Marianne S. Mast and others, "How Accurate Are Recruiters' First Impressions of Applicants in Employment Interviews?" *International Journal of Selection and Assessment* 19, no. 2 (2011): 206.

[9] Filip Lievens and Helga Peeters, "Interviewers' Sensitivity to Impression Management Tactics in Structured Interviews," *European Journal of Psychological Assessment* 24, no. 3 (2008): 179.

[10] Kareem Fahim, David Staba, and Alain Delaqueriere, "The Suspect in 3 Murders and 8 Rapes Blended In," *New York Times*, Jan. 18, 2007, B1.

[11] Ibid.

[12] Laura P. Naumann and others, "Personality Judgments Based on Physical Appearance," *Personality and Social Psychology Bulletin* 35, no. 12 (2009): 1670.

[13] Charles F. Bond and Bella M. DePaulo, "Accuracy of Deception Judgments," *Personality and Social Psychology Review* 10, no. 3 (2006): 215.

[14] Troy McMullen, "Dannon to Pay $45M to Settle Yogurt Lawsuit," last modified February 26, 2010, http://abcnews.go.com/Business/dannon-settles-lawsuit/story?id=9950269.

[15] "Dannon Agrees to Drop Exaggerated Health Claims for Activia Yogurt and DanActive Dairy Drink," last modified December 15, 2010, http://www.ftc.gov/opa/2010/12/dannon.shtm.

[16] Ibid., p. 216.

[17] Jeffrey Zaslow, "First Impressions Get Faster," *The Wall Street Journal* 247, no. 39 (2006): D4.

[18] Paul Ekman, *Emotions Revealed: Recognizing Faces and Feelings to Improve Communication and Emotional Life* (New York: Owl Books, Henry Holt and Company, LLC., 2003).

[19] Erving Goffman, *The Presentation of Self in Everyday Life* (New York: Doubleday, 1959).

[20] Michael A. Campion, David K. Palmer, and James E. Campion, "A Review of Structure in the Selection Interview," *Personnel Psychology* 50 (1997): 655-702; Jesus F. Salgado and Silvia Moscoso, "Comprehensive Meta-analysis of the Construct Validity of the Employment Interview," *European Journal of Work Organizational Psychology* 11 (2002): 299-324; Paul J. Taylor and Bruce Small, "Asking Applicants What They Would Do Versus What They Did Do: A Meta-analytic Comparison of Situational and Past Behaviour

Employment Interview Questions," *Journal of Occupational and Organizational Psychology* 75 (2002): 277-294.

[21] Jennifer Grasz, "Nearly Three-in-Ten Employers Have Caught a Fake Reference on a Job Application," last modified November 28, 2012, http://www.careerbuilder.com/share/aboutus/pressreleases detail.aspx?sd =11%2f28%2f2012&sc_cmp1=cb_pr727_&siteid =cbpr&id =pr727&ed= 12%2f31%2f2012.

[22] Lionel S. Lewis, "How Madoff Did It: Victims' Accounts," *Society* 48, no. 1 (2011): 70.

[23] Marianne S. Mast and others, "How Accurate Are Recruiters' First Impressions of Applicants in Employment Interviews?" *International Journal of Selection and Assessment* 19, no. 2 (2011): 200.

[24] Filip Lievens and Helga Peeters, "Interviewers' Sensitivity to Impression Management Tactics in Structured Interviews," *European Journal of Psychological Assessment* 24, no. 3 (2008): 174.

[25] Jennifer Grasz, "Nearly Three-in-Ten Employers Have Caught a Fake Reference on a Job Application," last modified November 28, 2012, http://www.careerbuilder.com/share/aboutus/pressreleases detail.aspx?sd= 11%2f28%2f2012&sc_cmp1=cb_pr727_&siteid =cbpr&id =pr727&ed= 12%2f31%2f2012.

[26] Charles F. Bond and Bella M. DePaulo, "Accuracy of Deception Judgments," *Personality and Social Psychology Review* 10, no. 3 (2006): 214-234.

[27] Stephen Porter and Leanne ten Brinke, "Dangerous Decisions: A Theoretical Framework for Understanding How Judges Assess Credibility in the Courtroom," *Law and Human Behavior* 14 (2009): 119-134; Albert Vrij, *Detecting Lies and Deceit: Pitfalls and Opportunities* (Chichester, UK: Wiley, 2008).

[28] Stephen Porter and others, "Is the Face a Window to the Soul? Investigation of the Validity of Intuitive Judgments of the Trustworthiness of Human Faces," *Canadian Journal of Behavioral Science* 40, no. 3 (2008): 171-177.

[29] Ibid., p. 211.

[30] Ibid., p. 10.

[31] Ibid., p. 9.

[32] Ann Rule, *The Stranger Beside Me* (New York: Pocket Books, 2009), 23.

[33] Ibid., p. 19.

[34] Ibid., p. 22.

[35] Monica J. Harris and Christopher P. Garris, "You Never Get a Second Chance to Make a First Impression: Behavioral Consequences of First Impressions," in *First Impressions*, eds. Nalini Ambady & John J. Skowronski (New York: The Guilford Press, 2008), 157.

[36] Frank R. Kardes, "When Should Consumers and Managers Trust Their Intuition?" *Journal of Consumer Psychology* 16, no. 1 (2006): 21.

[37] Heather M. Gray, "To What Extent, and Under What Conditions, are First Impressions Valid?" in *First Impressions*, eds. Nalini Ambady & John J. Skowronski (New York: The Guilford Press, 2008), 121.

[38] Ibid., p. 116.

[39] Monica J. Harris and Christopher P. Garris, "You Never Get a Second Chance to Make a First Impression: Behavioral Consequences of First Impressions," in *First Impressions*, eds. Nalini Ambady & John J. Skowronski (New York: The Guilford Press, 2008), 165.

[40] Julia Levashina and Michael A. Campion, "A Model of Faking Likelihood in the Employment Interview," *International Journal of Selection and Assessment* 14, no. 4 (2006): 299-316.

[41] Patrick Gallagher, William Fleeson, and Rick H. Hoyle, "A Self-Regulatory Mechanism for Personality Trait Stability: Contra-Trait Effort," *Social Psychological & Personality Science* 2, no. 4 (2011): 335-342.

[42] Heather M. Gray, "To What Extent, and Under What Conditions, are First Impressions Valid?" in *First Impressions*, eds. Nalini Ambady & John J. Skowronski (New York: The Guilford Press, 2008), 110.

[43] Eric D. Anderson and others, "Beliefs About Cues to Deception: Mindless Stereotypes or Untapped Wisdom?" *Journal of Nonverbal Behavior* 23, no. 1 (1999): 67-89.

[44] Ibid.

[45] John J. Skowronski and Donal E. Carlston, "Negativity and Extremity Biases in Impression Formation: A Review of Explanations," *Psychological Bulletin 105, no. 1 (1989):* 131.

[46] Robert Frick, "Why We Fall for Scams," *Kiplinger's Personal Finance* 65, no. 5 (2011): p. 24.

Chapter 9
Genuine Lasting Impressions

"Example is not the main thing in life – it is the only thing."[1]
– Albert Schweitzer

As I listened to Father George's comments from the pulpit, I realized once again how sincerely his remarks are delivered. Genuine people impress me the most and often their actions speak louder than words. Sometimes the truly humble don't say much at all, but speak through their example, their good deeds.

My friend, Rita, never said much but spoke through her generous deeds. For years Rita fashioned bracelets from beads. On several occasions she donated a thousand bracelets at a time for mission trips to Africa. Bracelets have also been distributed among poor families in Appalachia and in local nursing homes. Thousands of her bracelets have been handed out in the United States and throughout twenty-two countries in Africa.

Rita also crocheted many afghans over the years. Her crafts have been distributed among family members and area nursing homes. There are young girls in Mozambique, boys in Myanmar, women in Zimbabwe, older men in Kentucky, and elderly women in Napoleon, Ohio who are enjoying Rita's bracelets and afghans. Those gifts also came from their designer with a prayer. Her genuine lasting impression is generosity, as she has shared her talents and love with thousands of people she will never know.

Flashback – Genuine Inspirations

It is important to focus on the genuine impressions in life rather than fleeting first impressions. Since we can only rely on people whose behavior has revealed their true intentions in many encounters, we have no way of knowing whether a new acquaintance is behaving honestly. "Interestingly, the very situations where individuals try the hardest to impress are those where accurate impressions are most critical to the perceiver."[2] Therefore, deception is likely to be employed at the least opportune moment for the observer.

There are reasons to exercise a healthy dose of skepticism during a first encounter. Automobiles are routinely recalled for defects and toys often contain lead paint. Kids can't trust friends on the Internet and the rule preached by parents is "Don't talk to strangers". Entire neighborhoods are too dangerous for pizza delivery. Television commercials have seen a rise in promotions for computer security, identity theft protection, Angie's List of contractors, and the Better Business Bureau. Colleges are scrutinized through accreditation processes and products are tested by independent agencies such as Consumer Reports magazine.

A sure-fire indicator that deception is rampant is the growth of efforts to combat deceitful impressions. According to Information Age magazine, in the year 2008 there was an 11% annual growth in the worldwide information technology (IT) market for security software.[3] The world spending on security software reached $13.5 billion in 2012. It seems there is no shortage of scam artists, con men, deceivers, and people who worship the almighty dollar without regard for the impact of their behavior on others.

Few of us have the ability or the energy to play detective, so we learn to avoid a sales pitch from a stranger. We value the lasting impressions of those whose history with us demonstrates they are genuine. We can trust an impression which is based on multiple encounters of consistently reliable perceptions rather than risk deception from strangers. Genuine impressions, learned through multiple encounters, are truly appreciated.

One of the Best Companies

Google has again been chosen as the top choice in Fortune's 100 Best Companies to Work For.[4] This is their fifth time in the top spot in the last eight years and Google has been listed in the top four positions of company rankings for eight consecutive years. The 2013 survey included 259 firms in which more than 277,000 employees were surveyed. Ratings are based on responses to questions which measure management credibility, job satisfaction, compensation, hiring practices, communication, training, employee recognition, diversity efforts, and faith in management.[5]

Google is also one of the leading examples of corporate giving, as they have donated more than $100 million in grants in 2012.[6] Their efforts include four main priorities: 1) global impact, 2) disaster relief, 3) academic support, and 4) community affairs. Global efforts have linked technology and innovation to provide clean water, eliminate slavery, advance education, and protect endangered wildlife in developing countries. Their disaster relief contributions have shared the use of technology to support first responders of natural disasters, academic support has increased access to the world's information, and the community affairs focus supports the work of organizations in communities located near company offices. Theirs is truly a genuine lasting impression of corporate responsibility.

Genuine Impressions We Can Rely On

Once we become skeptical of our first impressions, we tend to prefer the long-term relationships in our lives. You may already be aware that many of those around us provide life lessons from which we have much to learn if we are only observant. It is beneficial to acknowledge and to appreciate their contributions to us. While they did not consciously strive to impress us, some people are so inspirational in their intentions and so genuine in their actions that their memories serve as cherished lasting impressions.

We can often point to a relative, friend, or co-worker as a lasting impression on our lives. At times it is a remembered saying which is timeless. Perhaps you have memorized an event which is commemorated at a holiday or other special occasion. You may even trace your career or other significant decision to a mentor's genuine influence.

The culmination of many experiences, like those which accumulate documentation over time to form a long-term memory, is an impression worth relying upon. Therefore, a genuine image observed in a variety of situations over a period of many years provides a valuable impression which is more worthy of confidence than any single observation. We learn to trust the business that consistently provides good service.

Satisfaction of Repeat Customers at Subway

The Subway restaurant chain was once again named the Harris Poll EquiTrend Quick Service Restaurant Brand of the Year in 2013. For the ninth year in a row, Subway has beaten all other fast food restaurants in a survey of 38,000 Americans as the Brand of the Year due to the loyalty of repeat customers.[7]

In a recent survey by Consumer Edge Insight, Subway was rated number one in great-tasting food and highest in customer intent to return.[8] The survey included of 3,000 consumers from a cross section of the U.S. adult population by age, gender, income, region, and ethnicity.[9]

As patrons frequently return to Subway, their perceptions of the restaurant chain are reaffirmed. Time and time again, customers' experiences reinforce a positive impression which confirms an accurate assessment of quality performance at all locations. As other studies have confirmed, multiple observations over a longer period of time in various settings lead customers to conclude they have experienced a genuine impression. Successful transactions in the long term reaffirm purchase decisions, as is true for the loyal customers of Subway.

Accuracy Over Time

Studies have found that additional information can be gathered and more accurate perceptions are reached when the observation time for judging a stranger is longer.[10] The shortest interval of observation might have allowed observers to correctly identify basic traits with some degree of confidence. However, longer exposures consistently lead to increased accuracy and each extension of viewing reduces the likelihood of a successful deception.

Reviews by friends who were well known by observers for a year or longer exhibited much higher levels of reliability compared with short-time observations by strangers. The opportunity to view a subject more frequently has been shown to provide a larger quantity of data, including a broader range of relevant information. "And as more relevant behavioral cues become available, the odds improve that the perceiver will actually detect some of these."[11] It is recommended that significant purchases and choices with long-term consequences should include multiple meetings before reaching a final decision.

Accuracy is enhanced when a person is observed in a variety of situations which test their reactions. Correct perceptions sometimes occur in brief viewings, but accuracy significantly improves with a greater number of observations and longer duration in a variety of settings. "The take-home message of these findings is that knowing someone longer is likely to allow you to judge him or her more accurately, but it is also important to observe that person in settings in which his or her personality has a chance to be expressed."[12]

America's Patriotic Flag Designer

Bob Heft was a friend of mine and a colleague, as he taught real estate classes for me at the college for twenty years. I don't believe most people truly appreciated the significance of Bob's accomplishments. As a high school student in 1958, he designed the fifty-star American flag for a history class project. When his flag was selected in 1960, Bob received a personal phone call from President Eisenhower inviting him to a ceremony to install the flag in Washington, DC.[13]

The flag designer later visited the White House fourteen times under nine presidents and toured several times with the Bob Hope show on USO tours to Vietnam. He was elected mayor of Napoleon, Ohio seven times, which attested to his popularity and success as a leader. Bob kept a busy speaking schedule, sometimes presenting 200 times per year. While he sometimes spoke at major universities and national events such as the bicentennial celebration, Bob most enjoyed talks to veterans groups and elementary school students.

I had the opportunity to see Bob present his story on more than one occasion, including a Constitution Day event at the College. It was fun to hear him tell the story of how he designed the flag, and his talk was also patriotic and inspirational. A variety of observations in different settings over many years had cemented my positive, genuine impression of Bob Heft.

Genuine Impression as a Long-Term Memory

Most of our lasting impressions, except for the one-time meeting with a stranger, are formed over a long period of time.

They represent the sum total of experiences which have been committed to a mental folder labeled long-term memory.

Until we are presented additional cues in future encounters with them, our first impression of strangers is our only impression. The brain temporarily stores that event in a mental folder labeled short-term memory. A long-term memory is only formed with the benefit of multiple experiences and a longer relationship which reinforces or refutes our first impression. Over the course of repeated encounters, what might be termed additional data points, we draw conclusions and map the trend of data which forms the long-term assessment.

Whether the product of a life-long relationship, a series of meetings, or a noteworthy one-time event, the final assessment of a person is the lasting impression they form for others. When additional encounters solidify the impression, it tends to be committed to long-term memory, what might be called their lasting impression.

The Trusted Voice of Television News

At a time when most Americans got their news by watching television, he was the most trusted voice in the country. Walter Cronkite "mastered the role of television news anchorman with such plain-spoken grace that he was called the most trusted man in America."[14] He was so popular that people often preferred to see him rather than the politicians he was interviewing. Cronkite had a knack for connecting with the American public.

Cronkite was legendary for realistic reporting on location. He crash-landed a glider in the Netherlands as a correspondent during World War II. Cronkite was one of eight journalists selected to accompany a bombing mission over Germany aboard a B-17 Flying Fortress. In later years Mr. Cronkite described how he manned a machine gun until he was up to his hips in spent shell casings.[15] In 1968 he reported about the Vietnam War after visiting the front lines.

When the Lunar Module touched down on the moon in 1969, Cronkite was nearly speechless in awe. Reporting that President Kennedy was assassinated in 1963, Cronkite paused to blink back tears. Walter Cronkite had been a reliable voice of news over three decades, earning the trust of Americans as a genuine impression of a nightly guest in the living room.

Loyalty in a Genuine Lasting Impression

Several years ago I drove a carload of friends to a golf outing. Midway through the trip, the two fellows in the back seat began debating whether I had made a wrong turn. After listening to their second guessing for several minutes, my friend, Wally, posed a question. "Larry is driving," he commented. "Why would you question where we are going?"

I later told Wally that his comment was truly a compliment of loyalty. He replied, "Well, I have faith in your decisions. And if you happened to make a wrong turn, I am okay going wherever you take me."

It seems to me that loyalty is a combination of confidence and trust, both of which require a long history. Wally and I have enjoyed a friendship and a mutual respect for many years. A genuine lasting impression only develops over time and the genuine impact trumps a first impression instinct.

Lasting Impression of the Fathers of Mercy

As I listened to the inspiration of Father George at the pulpit of the Chapel, I recalled the impact of missionaries and their legacy during a parish mission. At one of my visits with Father George I asked, "Do you ever consider that many who witness your mission will never see you again? I mean, I must be an unusual participant in that I have attended two of your missions and visited the Fathers of Mercy Chapel in Kentucky several times. The vast majority in your audience are likely seeing you for their first and last time during a mission, aren't they?"

"That is certainly true," Father George replied with a chuckle, "You might say you are a strange participant at your level of involvement. In most cases, people are seeing me as their only experience with a Fathers of Mercy mission. I have only one chance to impress them."

"Does your awareness of that 'one chance to impress' lead you to do anything special as you prepare for your mission talks?" I asked him.

"Certainly," he replied, "prior to each mission I pray for the guidance of the Holy Spirit and I take time to rehearse."

It occurred to me, as with most skills in life, that repetition leads to genuine improvement. With practice, one's golf game improves. Healthy eating habits lead to better health. The more often we demonstrate concern for others, the more likely that our genuine compassion will develop.

Father George continued to address the audience gathered for the memorial service at the Chapel, "The legacy of Dr. Zach's book promotes a genuine lasting impression as an influence on others, as it did near the end of one man's life. I am certain Dr. Zach would like me to share with you the rest of the story."

We should appreciate the value of genuine lasting impressions!

---

[1] Albert Schweitzer, *"Thoughts for Our Times,"* ed. Erica Anderson (Mount Vernon, NY: Peter Pauper Press, 1975), 51.

[2] Lauren J. Human and others, "Your Best Self Helps Reveal Your True Self: Positive Self-Presentation Leads to More Accurate Personality Impressions," *Social Psychological and Personality Science* 3, no. 1 (2012): 23.

[3] J.J. Robinson, "Security in the Spotlight, " last modified January 23, 2009, http://www.information-age.com/channels/security-and-continuity/perspectives-and-trends/990012/security-in-the-spotlight.html.

[4] "Fortune 100 Best Companies to Work For: Google," accessed August 23, 2013, http://money.cnn.com/magazines/fortune/best-companies/2013/snapshots/1.html.

[5] Robert Levering and Milton Moskowitz, "100 Best Companies to Work For: How We Pick the 100 Best," August 23, 2013, http://money.cnn.com/magazines/fortune/best-companies/2013/faq/index.html?iid=bc.

[6] "Google Giving," August 23, 2013, http://www.google.com/giving/.

[7] "2013 Harris Poll EquiTrend Rankings," accessed July 19, 2013, http://www.harrisinteractive.com/Insights/EquiTrendRankings.aspx.

[8] Dale Buss, "McDonald's Brand Strength Keeps Its U.S. Customers Coming Back for More," modified January 21, 2013, http://www.brandchannel.com/home/post/2013/01/21/McDonalds-Satisfaction-Survey-012113.aspx.

[9] "Consumer Edge Insight's Restaurant Demand Tracker," accessed July 27, 2013, http://consumeredgeinsight.com/trackers/industry/restaurants.

[10] Dana R. Carney, C. Randall Colvin, and Judith A. Hall, "A Thin Slice Perspective on the Accuracy of First Impressions," *Journal of Research in Personality* 41, no. 5 (2007): 1054-1072.

[11] Melinda C. Blackman and David C. Funder, "The Effect of Information on Consensus and Accuracy in Personality Judgment," *Journal of Experimental Social Psychology* 34 (1998): 166.

[12] David C. Funder, "Accurate Personality Judgment," *Current Directions in Psychological Science* 21, no. 3 (2012): 180.

[13] Frederick N. Rasmussen, "A Half-Century Ago, New 50-Star American Flag Debuted in Baltimore," last modified July 2, 2010, http://articles.baltimoresun.com/2010-07-02/news/bs-md-backstory-1960-flag-20100702_1_48-star-flag-blue-canton-fort-mchenry.

[14] Douglas Martin, "Walter Cronkite, 92, Dies; Trusted Voice of TV News," last modified July 17, 2009, http://www.nytimes.com/2009/07/18/us/18cronkite.html?pagewanted=all.

[15] Walter Cronkite, IV & Maurice Isserman, *Cronkite's War:His World War II Letters Home* (Washington: National Geographic Society, 2013), 57.

Chapter 10
Lasting Impression As A Legacy

"A hundred times every day I remind myself that my inner and outer life depend on the labours of other men, living and dead, and that I must exert myself in order to give in the same measure as I have received and am still receiving."[1] – Albert Einstein

I recall people during my lifetime whose impression is true generosity. "Benefit Tonight - Shalom Project at St. John's UCC," was the recent message on the sign in front of the local pizza restaurant. The manager hosts a fundraiser for almost any charity. Employees volunteer their labor and a percentage of sales goes toward a good cause. There is usually a raffle drawing for prizes, creating a festive atmosphere. Although the restaurant is located in a small town, many outsiders as well as local residents turn out for each charitable event. The long-term impression of patrons is a positive outlook toward a caring business. Customers frequently return to the restaurant which promotes local compassion.

The amazing effect of generosity is that it becomes contagious. Like the patrons at pizza restaurant fundraisers, people follow the example of others who are charitable. The message of helping people in need continues to inspire others. In economics there is a concept called the "multiplier effect", which essentially means the ongoing effect of new spending throughout the economy as it is respent over and over to multiply the effect of the original spending. The "multiplier effect" of generosity replays charity over and over, becoming a legacy of the person whose generosity inspired others.

Flashback – A Legacy of Generosity

I once visited Hershey, Pennsylvania and toured Hershey's Chocolate World, where the company story is told. Milton S. Hershey began to manufacture chocolate in 1894 in rural Pennsylvania where he was born and where he knew he could access an adequate supply of fresh milk produced on local dairy farms. The company was a huge success, but workers were scarce in farm country. Hershey built a new factory and designed a town around it to provide a place for employees to live close to their jobs. He included tree-lined streets as well as a bank, school, and parks.

Success led to a history of philanthropy as the legacy of Milton Hershey. "Mr. Hershey's belief that an individual is morally obligated to share the fruits of success with others resulted in significant contributions to society. Together with his wife, Catherine, he established the most prominent of his philanthropic endeavors, the Hershey Industrial School."[2] Milton and Catherine Hershey founded a school for orphaned boys because they had no children. Hershey applied his chocolate fortune toward two main projects: 1) the town of Hershey and 2) his school.

In the 1930's Mr. Hershey kept employees busy as they constructed a community building with two elegant theatres, an addition to the boys' school, and an arena. It was a great source of personal pride that no workers lost their jobs at Hershey's company during the Depression years, as employees were kept on the payroll by temporarily enhancing the town for the benefit of all citizens when there was reduced demand for chocolate. An organization that produces a quality product, takes care of employees, and serves its community is truly an inspiring legacy to all.

Relying on a Legacy of Trust

It is natural for humans to review the consequences of previous decisions and to prefer those whose impressions have proven to be trustworthy. Repeat customers appreciate the positive legacy of satisfaction with a product or service that has consistently proven to be worthwhile. They become loyal customers when the impression of a business is a positive legacy which encourages them to return over and over.

Patterns of effective decisions lead us to increasingly appreciate continuous relationships and the lasting wisdom provided by those around us through multiple encounters over a long term. You may be able to recognize the lasting impact others have provided through many experiences. Each of us also influences others by the impressions we communicate to them. The legacy we leave to others is part of the ongoing "circle of life", as we grow to become parents and then grandparents just as those who passed before us.[3] This is the ongoing process of benefiting from a legacy, and then determining our own legacy, as the lasting impression we genuinely live creates a valuable impact on others from examples we've been provided.

Inspiring Legacies

Many famous figures in history have presented a legacy by words and by deeds. Green Bay Packers coach, Vince Lombardi, inspired successful teams for years through his leadership. He also instilled traits in his players which have persisted long after Coach Lombardi passed away. His legacy is preserved in many quotes.

"Perfection is not attainable, but if we chase perfection we can catch excellence," said Lombardi.[4] "Individual commitment to a group effort – that is what makes a team work, a company work, a society work, a civilization work."[5] Lombardi shared specific advice about our lasting impression, "After all the cheers have died down and the stadium is empty, after the headlines have been written, and after you are back in the quiet of your room and the championship ring has been placed on the dresser and after all the pomp and fanfare have faded, the enduring thing that is left is the dedication to doing with our lives the very best we can to make the world a better place in which to live."[6]

Winston Churchill inspired the world at a dark time with many speeches. Some are well known inspirations to others. "How else can we put ourselves in harmonious relation with the great verities and consolations of the infinite and the eternal?" "There is nothing that helps a man in his conduct through life more than a knowledge of his own characteristic weaknesses (which, guarded against, become his strength)."[7]

Rev. Billy Graham has inspired millions with his presentations and his advice. "Our days are numbered. One of the primary goals in our lives should be to prepare for our last day. The legacy we leave is not just in our possessions, but in the quality of our lives."[8] Figures such as Vince Lombardi, Winston Churchill, Billy Graham, and many others have left inspirational messages that empower us. They provide powerful legacies to guide each of us as we proceed on our own individual journeys through life.

A Legacy of Philanthropy

The Bill and Melinda Gates Foundation strives to unlock the potential inside every individual. "We believe by doing these things – focusing on a few big goals and working with our partners on innovative solutions – we can help every person get the chance to live a healthy, productive life."[9] The foundation targets two primary issues, which are: 1) poverty and poor health in developing countries and 2) the failure of American education.

In 2010 Warren Buffett, Melinda Gates, and Bill Gates announced "The Giving Pledge", in which they "encourage

America's wealthiest families to donate the majority of their wealth to philanthropic causes and charities."[10] The foundation currently holds an endowment of $38 billion and has distributed payments of $28 billion since its inception. The practice of being charitable truly demonstrates awareness of the philosophy that "more will be demanded of the person entrusted with more" (from Luke 12:48)[11] A legacy of wealthy donors is the thousands of beneficiaries whose quality of life was improved by generosity.

The Old Man and His Grandson

The following tale is attributed to the Brothers Grimm, but the story has been retold in other printings as well:

A frail old man went to live with his son, daughter-in-law, and four year-old grandson. The old man's hands trembled, his eyesight was blurred, and his step faltered. The family ate together at the table, but the elderly grandfather's shaky hands and failing sight made eating difficult. Peas rolled off his spoon onto the floor. When he grasped the glass, milk spilled on the tablecloth. The son and daughter-in-law became irritated with the mess.

"We must do something about father," said the son. "I've had enough of his spilled milk, noisy eating, and food on the floor."

So the husband and wife set a small table in the corner. There, the grandfather ate alone while the rest of the family enjoyed dinner. Since the grandfather had broken a dish or two, his food was served in a wooden bowl.

When the family glanced in the grandfather's direction, sometimes he had a tear in his eye as he sat alone. Still, the only words the couple had for him were sharp admonitions when he dropped a fork or spilled food.

The four-year-old watched it all in silence. One evening before supper, the father noticed his son playing with wood scraps on the floor. He asked the child, "What are you making?"

The boy responded, "Oh, I am making a little bowl for you and Mama to eat your food in when I grow up." The four year-old smiled and went back to work.

The words so struck the parents that they were speechless. Then tears started to stream down their cheeks. Though no word was spoken, both knew what must be done. That evening the husband took the grandfather's hand and gently led him back to the family table. For the remainder of his days he ate every meal with the family on the same china plates. For some reason, neither husband nor wife seemed to care any longer when a fork was dropped, milk spilled, or the tablecloth soiled.

The example of family togetherness had been initiated by the youngest and least expected of the family members. Once inspired, the parents were motivated to include the whole family at mealtime, a legacy likely to become a family tradition to be followed into future generations around the dinner table.[12]

Mother Teresa of Calcutta

She is so small in stature as to be nearly invisible, so meek of voice that she is almost unheard, but so powerful in deeds that her legacy resonates around the world. Mother Teresa had created the most genuine of impressions by her example. While most people avoided the poor, sick, and diseased population of India, she went to live among them, assisting and comforting the poorest in society. While her intent was not to be noticed, it was impossible to overlook her works of mercy in a difficult location. Even a bustling world had to pause for a moment to comprehend the unselfish acts of a small elderly nun.

"A survey conducted in India in the autumn of 2002 ranked Mother Teresa as the 'Greatest Indian' since independence", which is interesting because Mother Teresa is not originally from India.[13] However, her legacy is that she continues to inspire others.

"Mother is a symbol of love and compassion. Her life of loving service to the poor has inspired many to follow the same path."[14]

Legacies of Experience Are Not Immediately Appreciated

Over the years I have observed numerous situations in which younger people became frustrated with older people. They are certain that older folks are too old fashioned. The elders drive too slowly, they talk too much, and they spend a lot of time with other old people. They oppose change. Their opinions are often underappreciated.

Older people view the young upstarts as brash and careless in their behavior and crude in their language. The younger generation drives too fast and behaves selfishly. They are viewed by their elders as wanting to change everything. At age 18, a person has zero years of adulthood. They have not worked at a serious job and they have shouldered few responsibilities. They clamor for change to a better situation of income and recognition.

An interesting transformation occurs as people age. The younger folks begin to drive more carefully over time and speak with caution, as they become parents with concern for the well-being of children, friends, and colleagues. Hectic lives lead them to appreciate slower, quieter music with enchanting melodies and inspiring lyrics. They learn to appreciate carefully crafted foods which require deliberate efforts of baking rather than fast food options.

As they become more experienced, the younger crowd learns to buy groceries, pay electric bills, work responsibly, make mortgage payments, and juggle busy schedules. They learn to handle success as well as adversity. As they mature, their generation recognizes lasting impressions which provided true legacies. They also become a lasting influence on the next generation.

Legacy of Temptation

Sometimes life's legacies are not created by heroes performing significant positive accomplishments. A legacy can be created through negative behavior which then resonates through others as a warning. On October 6, 2011 a car driven by Brandie ran a stop sign and hit Carol's car broadside. The force of that collision killed Carol instantly and caused her husband serious injuries. Brandie was behind the wheel even though her license had been suspended. Her prior drinking convictions had resulted in jail sentences and several terms on probation.

The crash had immediately impacted several families and many more friends, neighbors, and relatives with the wrong kind of legacy. People were quick to ask, "Why does God allow evil to happen?"

As Father George explains in his mission talk, "God can only permit what is universally good."[15] We may not understand the plan, but we can be assured that every action, each event, occurs because it contributes toward what is universally good. It is one of the few answers that can help us make sense of the situation.

Since the "universal good" is elusive, the answer must be in the ensuing effect. The auto accident which killed one woman was the precipitating event which finally took Brandie out of the driver's seat for a sentence of three to fifteen years in prison.[16] It may have saved her three elementary school daughters from a future deadly collision. Maybe other drivers are now spared from a similar fate, since Brandie is no longer driving. There might be others who were themselves reckless drinkers, but have now been shocked sober by the consequences of this crash and the penalty for this driver. Perhaps other young people were on a course of self-destructive behavior, but are moved by this devastation to modify their lives.

Carol had worked as a school secretary for thirty years, but she didn't just staff the office. When students called in sick, she would phone them at home to check on their progress. Carol watched to make certain kids had coats and gloves. She tracked down the owners when items were left in the lost and found pile. Carol was also quick to help relatives and neighbors, baking a dish for funeral dinners and helping anyone in need. She had touched so many lives in such numerous ways that a steady stream of mourners filed through the funeral home for hours.

If this tragedy really is part of a plan which is "universally good", then it would never be effective if the victim was less surprising. If a nasty person had been killed, people would just think, "He deserved what he got." When a less careful person suffers a dreadful fate, people think "It may be her own fault." However, when a saintly person is taken, it becomes a cause to reflect. It is a true learning opportunity for everyone.

In the end the car crash is a tragedy for all involved, including the victim, her family, neighbors, friends, the guilty offender, and the perpetrator's family. All are suffering. The only good that may occur is the legacy of a life-altering epiphany which causes others to straighten the course of their lives. The "universal good" is likely to be the motivation which will lead others to appreciate their time on earth, influence people to end their destructive habits, and inspire them toward better behavior.

Brandie is really not that different from the rest of us. In spite of her actions, she is not inherently evil. Her actions were triggered by a moment of weakness that she surely wishes could be replayed differently. As philosopher Peter Kreeft described, "we learn from the mistakes we make and the suffering they bring."[17] As I once heard a minister advise, the lesson of tragedy is the need for grace in our lives to overcome a negative legacy.

The Grandmother Test

Whenever I see people misbehaving, communicating a truly negative impression, I recall what a friend once termed the "Grandmother Test." Our poor judgment may not always be obvious to us, but there is a quick method to determine if we are out of line. We only have to ask ourselves one question, "Is this the kind of behavior that would make grandmother proud?"

Within one moment, we can judge our decisions and recalibrate our lives. Whether grandma is alive or not, no matter how far away she might be, we can rely upon our memory of her to guide us. I suspect even grandpa might have applied this strategy on more than one occasion to review his own decisions.

If we consider the impact of our choices on family members, we may spare ourselves embarrassment. We might also keep our family from feeling disappointed. There are times that each of us can benefit from the "Grandmother Test", relying on a time tested standard which keeps us from developing a negative legacy.

The Power of Example

It is true that the one chance encounter with an inspirational man in Washington, DC had impacted me by his concern for others. I am still witnessing the power of his example as good deeds are noticed and then replicated by others. The legacy of the Park Service employee becomes more vivid with each additional example of generosity that I see performed by people around me.

Father George continued, "The main point of a legacy is not for people who perform good deeds to be honored, but for others to notice the good works and then, in turn, to repeat the observed compassion as they then help others in need. It becomes like the "handing off of the baton" in life's relay race in which each of us who becomes aware of lasting impressions is handed the baton of compassion. Their influence is passed to others, as one good deed begets another, continuing the chain reaction of a legacy. We now honor one who has finished that race and handed off the baton of lasting impressions to us as his legacy."

A lasting impression is a powerful legacy!

---

[1] Albert Einstein, *The World As I See It* (translated by Alan Harris), (London: J. Lane, 1935), 1.

[2] "Milton the Man" accessed July 3, 2013, http://www.miltonhershey.com/milton_knowledge.html.

[3] Roger Allers and Rob Minkoff, (Directors), "*The Lion King*", recorded 1994. Disney, DVD.

[4] John Eisenberg, *That First Season* (New York: Houghton Mifflin Harcourt Publishing, 2009), 76.

[5] Ibid.

[6] Family of Vince Lombardi, "Famous Quotes by Vince Lombardi," accessed April 14, 2013, http://www.vincelombardi.com/quotes.html.

[7] A.W. Hall, *Great Thoughts From Master Minds* (London: Smith Publishing Company, Vol. V, 1908), 168.

[8] Billy Graham, *Hope for the Troubled Heart: Finding God in the Midst of Pain* (New York: Bantam Books, 1993), 192.

[9] Bill Gates and Melinda Gates, "Letter From Bill and Melinda Gates" accessed August 23, 2013, http://www.gatesfoundation.org/Who-We-Are/General-Information/Letter-from-Bill-and-Melinda-Gates.

[10] "A Tradition of Giving," accessed August 23, 2013, http://www.gatesfoundation.org/Who-We-Are/General-Information/History.

[11] United States Conference of Catholic Bishops, *The New American Bible* (Washington: United States Conference of Catholic Bishops, 2002), 1116.

[12] Jacob L. C. Grimm and Wilhelm C. Grimm, *Children's and Household Tales* (Kassel, Germany: Grimm Brothers, 1812), Tale 78.

[13] Kathryn Spink, *Mother Teresa: An Authorized Biography* (New York: Harper Collins, 2011), 294.

[14] Ibid., p. 297.

[15] Fr. George McInnis, *"Christ Our God, Truth Incarnate" DVD,* Fathers of Mercy, 2010.

[16] Dennis Pelham, "Driver Gets Prison for Crash That Killed Community Leader," *Daily Telegram,*
December 15, 2012, 1.

[17] Lee Strobel, *The Case for Faith* (Grand Rapids, MI: Zondervan, 2000), 41.

Chapter 11
Planning Your Family Legacy

"The legacy of heroes is the memory of a great name and the inheritance of a great example."

– Benjamin Disraeli[1]

I recently heard an insightful quote in a television commercial for New York Life Insurance. The message was, "We are all reflections of the people who came before us. The good they did inspires us, prepares us, and guides us."[2] That statement sums up the impact of a legacy which lives beyond ancestors and influences future generations. Living that legacy, we become their reflection.

I have tried my hand at creating a long-term impact. I hope this book will persuade others to consider their own legacies. If truly inspired, they will pass along a wealth of information, as well as the goal for others to create a legacy in their own lives.

We Can Each Become a Legacy

If we watch closely, we will realize through life's everyday events how each of us has been influenced. In turn, we can also recognize how we have impacted others through our legacy for them. The lyrics of the song "For Good" in the Broadway play, Wicked, explain how we leave an impression on those we encounter. "Because I knew you, I have been changed."[3] I can't think of a more powerful testimonial or a more sincere way to thank a close friend for the inspiration provided by their legacy.

A true legacy is an event which inspires and motivates others. There are numerous people who have provided me with a remembrance of an earlier time or a significant event. At that moment they were surely unaware that I might latch onto their stories as legacies. Had they known my memory was in record mode, is that the impression they would have chosen? Is there a different memory they might have preferred to be remembered?

You may recall positive and negative impressions of others that have been committed to long-term memory, and then realize that their life experiences have actually created legacies for us. Just as those who have impressed us, each of us also projects a legacy to others – sometimes positive, and in other cases negative. This realization often leads us to first fear, then to comprehend, and later to appreciate the ability to create a legacy. We can help others with our effort to determine an individual legacy. If you choose to develop that legacy, you get to design the type of impact which will leave a lasting impression on others around us and lessons which may benefit them.

The Clock Is Ticking On Our Legacies

We may feel an interest in determining a legacy, but fail to act on it. People often have good intentions to accomplish life's goals.[4] Drivers urge a dwindling gas tank to go one more mile, although the fuel gauge suggests otherwise. Partyers plan to go home after one last drink, although the "one for the road" is the most dangerous. Gamblers insist on placing one last bet before going home, but then stay long enough to give back everything they have won. Smokers frequently light up "one last time" and dieters vow to begin a diet after one last dessert. Family members decide to communicate how they really feel at the next holiday. Lukewarm Christians promise that next Sunday is the day their conversion will begin.

However, none of us knows for certain if we have one more mile, one last drink, one more bet, one more holiday, or one more Sunday to enjoy. If we die unexpectedly, that last message never gets delivered or the conversion never occurs. It happens all too often that our best intentions are not fulfilled. With foresight we can not only plan ahead, but determine events which will occur after we are gone. We can create our lasting impression and define our continuing impact on others.

According to author Jim Rohn, leaving a legacy is a responsibility we owe to others who follow us:

"The legacy we leave is part of the ongoing foundations of life. Those who came before leave us the world we live in. Those who will come after will have only what we leave them. It is an act of responsibility to leave a legacy. Because of the power of our lives and the legacies we leave, it is a great responsibility to choose to leave a positive legacy. All good men and women must take responsibility to create legacies that will take the next generation to a level we could only imagine. Purposefully leaving a legacy for others breaks the downward pull of selfishness that can be inherent in us. When we strive to leave a legacy, we are acting with a selflessness that can only be good for us."[5]

The effort to inform and inspire others can pay dividends, "for a person will reap only what he sows" (from Galatians, 6:7).[6] The main question is, "Will we take advantage of the opportunity to form our legacy which inspires others?"

Almost A Legacy

For several years I had consciously selected a few families to visit during the Christmas season. They were elderly couples who lived plainly and seemed to lack visitors. It was easy for me to drop off a basket of fruit and goodies to Ray and Pauline, as they had sold us our first house when Alice and I got married. Besides,

Ray had always been a colorful guy and a hard worker for the local American Legion post. It was enlightening to hear events he recalled from his days as a soldier in World War II and as a businessman during subsequent years. They were appreciative of my visits and I enjoyed interesting talks each time I stopped to see them.

The last season I visited, Ray and I talked about my father who had died twenty years earlier. Ray told me he had known my father's family and could show me exactly where my father had lived at several locations during his early years, as well as my grandfather before him, and we agreed that I would drive him to those places when we had better weather in the spring. However, before we could visit those sites of my ancestors, Ray passed away that winter. I had missed another wonderful opportunity to learn family history.

A Spontaneous Wedding Legacy

When my wife and I received an invitation to the wedding of our friends' son, it was an occasion we needed to attend. I had worked with Rick at the college and Deb is a good friend. Their family had been at our house years earlier. We looked forward to attending the event.

The church glowed with just enough candlelight to illuminate our path. The combination of candles and piano music provided an amazing ambience and the wedding was very beautiful.

Afterward a huge white tent hosted the outdoor reception and tables were decorated with a variety of flowers. A generator powered the food tables and the music DJ, while guests enjoyed perfect weather.

We visited with Rick and Deb at the reception, as well as their twin sons, Steve, the groom, and Adam, who was the best man. Rick commented that Adam is Mr. Happy-go-Lucky, while Steve is Mr. Serious. "They are different as night and day," Rick explained. "Adam is always laughing, while Steve hardly ever smiles." He was right about the boys. Adam was quick to laugh during conversations and frequently smiled. However, Steve didn't even grin during the toast or when his father presented a gag gift to Steve's bride, Whitney.

Once the meal, the cake cutting ceremony, and the tossing of the bouquet were concluded, the DJ announced that dancing would soon begin. We were ready to leave, but wanted to watch the father-bride dance and the mother-groom dance. As the wedding party and parents surrounded the dance floor, the DJ took up his microphone. Photographers stood at attention and guests scurried off the dance floor.

"We will now have the bride and her father come forward to dance," the DJ announced, and a watery-eyed dad held his newly married little girl. As the music ended, the DJ called out, "Okay, then, everyone is invited to the dance floor!"

I told Alice, "He didn't even have the mother dance with the groom."

I stood and walked to the dance floor. Shaking hands with Steve, I thanked him, "We're leaving now, but we appreciate the chance to be with you today. By the way, you should ask your mother to dance. She looks great tonight." I patted him on the back, then walked back to our table. As we started toward our car, I looked over my shoulder to see Steve dancing with his mother. I motioned to him with the "thumbs up" sign and waived to Steve, who flashed a rare grin from ear to ear. As the photographer caught on and hurried to get the picture, I realized that I may have just helped the newlyweds to create a photo memory. Wedding pictures of Steve and Whitney will include the mother-groom dance after all. It occurred to me later that I might have helped create a legacy of Steve and Whitney's wedding celebration.

Need for a Legacy

According to author Stephen Covey, "the need to leave a legacy is our spiritual need to have a sense of meaning, purpose, personal congruence, and contribution."[7] The drive to create a legacy is not simply a selfish event, it is not an attempt to immortalize oneself. I guess it would be exactly that if you spent money to erect a statue of your own image or if you bought naming rights for a building or a stadium. However, those whose contributions are truly recognized as a legacy are remembered as significant for their helpful impact on those who have been inspired.

A true legacy is formed with the intent of informing or encouraging others. A legacy has been defined as "something transmitted by or received from an ancestor or predecessor from the past."[8] When contemplating how you might frame your legacy, consider the question, "If you found yourself on your deathbed, what would you most regret not having done during your life" and how would you most want to be remembered?[9]

Creating Our Legacy

One author has researched the formation of legacies and identified characteristics of those who strive to create a legacy.[10] Alexa Ispas has proposed that legacy creators are able to consciously impact others as they endeavor:

1. to focus on the important and the durable.
2. to not let themselves be distracted by the short-term.
3. to work towards creating legacy every single day.
4. to avoid making excuses for not creating legacy, to themselves or others.
5. not to postpone creating legacy. The time is now.
6. never to be entirely happy with what they have achieved. To always strive for more.

7. to make do with what they have in creating legacy.
8. to collaborate with the best possible people.
9. not to shy away from discomfort and sacrifice.
10. not be afraid to make mistakes.
11. to learn from mistakes.
12. not to be afraid of losing everything and starting back at square one.
13. to remember the people who helped them.
14. to reject mediocrity, regardless of peer pressure.
15. to eliminate the people who hold them back.
16. to always change when they think they know something.
17. to honor and cherish their body. Not to drive themselves to the brink of insanity.
18. not to shy away from the impossible.
19. not to give in to peer pressure.
20. to be kind to the people around them, even when under pressure.
21. to work their socks off.

Observations of legacies among friends, have led me to focus on a few key topics as a start toward forming a legacy:

1. Family Focus   – personal budget
                         – life insurance
                         – financial records
                         – legacy of parents
                         – inheritance
                         – family histories
                         – traditions
                         – messages to others

2. Professionalism   – a legacy of quality circles
                                               – the value of work
                                             – importance of mentors
                                             – servant leadership
                                             – a legacy of encouragement
                                             – leading with respect
                                             – honesty and integrity
                                             – true commitment
                                             – the addition business

3. Spirituality   – spiritual quotes
                                             – the case for Christianity
                                             – contagious charity
                                             – the prodigal son
                                             – forgiveness
                                             – inspiring young legacies
                                             – a spiritual investment
                                             – our individual faith journeys
                                             – one man's epiphany
                                             – an extra kick at the end of the race

While most people think they are focused on things that are first in life, "perhaps they would be better off concentrating on things that are last."[11] We would each be well served to remember that there is no time like the present to begin our legacy quest.

Family Focus

I recently watched a 1963 episode of Bonanza on television which was focused on the legacy of families. Ben Cartright (Lorne Greene) advised a suspicious companion, "The only thing that we leave behind in this world when we die is our children," he explained. "They become the way we are remembered."[12]

By the end of the show, Ben Cartright's relationship with his three sons had persuaded the adversary to make the right decisions regarding his own sons. Good had triumphed over evil.

"You've made the right decision," Ben Cartright explained, "and the legacy of your sons will be a compliment to you."

Those without children are typically even less aware that their impact on nieces and nephews, as well as friends and neighbors, can be a significant legacy of their lives. They may not observe their effect on others around them, but "the inheritance of a great example" is not limited to members of one's immediate family.[13]

Personal Budget

I can recall that my parents were thrifty when I was growing up. One vivid memory is that we ate Quaker puffed wheat cereal which was poured from a plastic bag and added our own sugar instead of buying the sweetened cereal in a box. Getting shiny shoes and different clothes was a seasonal event attached to the start of school. For several years I actually thought that you could only buy new clothes in August.

I remember sitting in front of my dad's chair to watch television on Sunday nights after taking a bath because the rug in front of the chair was warmer than the linoleum floor. I don't recall that we went without anything, but we were certainly frugal. Financial responsibility is not an instinct that we possess at birth. Most of us need lessons and role models we can emulate to achieve financial stability.

Money management is an important skill to instill in heirs. A successful plan to manage finances begins with a budget. As stated by Dave Ramsey, "A budget is people telling their money where to go instead of wondering where it went."[14] The chart in Appendix A, Personal Budget, is a start toward identifying actual spending compared with your spending plan. It also reveals how spending compares with take home pay, hopefully identifying that the actual allocation of money is less than the amount of revenue.

Life Insurance

A review of insurance is worthwhile for several reasons. The exercise will: 1) identify an adequate amount of life insurance, 2) reflect on the expected cost of funeral services, and 3) determine beneficiaries and contingent beneficiaries of policies. Over the years I had accumulated several life insurance policies, a combination of whole life and term life. Some were purchased, others were related to employment, and still others are attached to retirement benefits. I finally got around to summarizing all of my policies into a spreadsheet of information. You may find it helpful to consider a sample spreadsheet template provided for your use in Appendix B, Life Insurance Summary.

Financial Records

It is important to share financial records and documents with those who are close to you. Information regarding bank accounts, real estate deeds, vehicle titles, and loan documents is important, as well as the location of bank accounts, stocks and bonds, and safe deposit boxes so that they can be accessed.

When my uncle Jake died, we all wondered if there were secret locations where he might have stored sports memorabilia. Safe deposit boxes somewhere might have housed baseball cards and the most precious autographed baseballs. However, he had told nobody about them, so we are all left wondering.

A sample spreadsheet template is provided for your use in Appendix C, Financial Records. That information will be very helpful to your heirs and they will not have to wonder what might have been.

Legacy of Parents

When I reminisced with a colleague about our former coworker, Jeff, I remembered seeing a thank-you note he had written to the local tire dealer. "Thanks so much for repairing my flat tire" was the message pinned to the bulletin board along with Jeff's business card. I don't think the tire shop gets many thank-you notes, so Jeff's card was posted for all to see.

"You know why Jeff wrote notes, don't you?" my colleague, Jason, asked. "He once told me that his mother taught him to thank people with a card whenever he received a kindness as a child. The practice stuck with him, and I often saw him at his desk after hours writing thank-you notes. He enjoyed thanking people."

"I recall receiving one of Jeff's cards at the college," I replied. "What a wonderful impression of gratitude from Jeff's mother is being passed along to others through him."

My friend, Louie, exemplifies how we communicate a legacy through our children. Louie is passionate about life; he works hard and he plays hard. However, he always found time for his children. I remember him coaching Serena in junior girls' softball and he coached Alex for several years in baseball. Serena's high school basketball team was the runner-up in the state basketball tournament in two of her four high school years, winning all but the final game. Alex's high school basketball team was also a finalist, losing only the last game of the tournament. I have to believe that Louie had an influence on their passion for the game.

The dedication Louie showed his children is an example of passing along a work ethic and a desire to win. However, his most important legacy, the lesson to others, is the attention he showered on his kids. Each of us should live our lives as models for others and at least consider that "actions speak louder than words."

As referenced earlier, there is a "circle of life", a continuous passing of the torch from one generation to the next, as we foster a legacy through our example for others to follow.[15] I have written a poem which captures the essence of life's legacies which we receive from our ancestors and which are then forwarded on to our heirs and friends in a continuous cycle:

Thank Your Parents

When you find yourself working while others may play
And you've something to show for your use of the day,
        Thank your parents.

If your vocation in life over many a year,
Is not just a job, but a thriving career,
        Thank your parents.

When charity is learned both in word and in deed
And you're helping your neighbor when you see a need,
        Thank your parents.

If you take time to worship, reflect, and to hear
What your Maker has taught you each week of the year,
        Thank your parents.

When your sons and your daughters seek you for advice,
Value your wisdom, and view you as nice,
        They're thanking the parents.

For their job is beginning, it's their turn to stress,
Over their sons' and daughters' future lives of success,
        They're now the parents.

Inheritance

You might consider writing a last will to communicate intentions for the disbursement of property after you are gone. A conscious decision on your part will alleviate disagreements which may occur without the benefit of your direct involvement. This is especially true if there are family heirlooms or possessions with sentimental value. A statement in your will can assure transfer of property according to your desire or a prior discussion.

The process of contemplating inheritance issues will assure that a guardian will be determined for young children. A will can also address expenses to raise surviving dependents and how those costs will be covered. As with most decisions, consideration in advance will occur at a time of greater logic and rational thinking with a minimum of emotional interference.

Unfortunately, most of us postpone planning for end of life events. "Many of us put off facing the necessities connected with the last day of one's life – namely the making out of a last will and testament."[16] A sample spreadsheet template is provided in Appendix D, Inheritance Summary. A review of inheritance decisions is important for several reasons. The exercise will: 1) identify property to be transferred, 2) cause you to reflect on the recipients of possessions, and 3) provide peace of mind that your heirs are determined and your wishes are fulfilled.

Family Histories

A few years ago, I had a chance to appreciate an effort to capture family history which I observed in my friend, Jon. His family had printed a book to collect together recipes entitled The Call Family Favorite Recipes. Each family member was invited to submit a recipe recalled from earlier days when their mother, aunt, or grandmother had demonstrated her cooking skills. It was a wonderful remembrance of food, which has been identified as a powerful cue of memories.[17] As each relative recalled the recipe for a special dish, it would jog the memory of related events in their lives. Interestingly, those food memories also inspired the recollection of family events and triggered the opportunity to retell those stories to another generation.

The project resulted in a cookbook to assist the culinary skills of family members. Relatives were drawn together in a manner that could not have otherwise occurred. The culmination of the Call recipes allows them to eat their way through family history and to share family relationships which have become much more powerful than the printing of a recipe book. The legacy of their family cooking is a project which honors the memory of ancestors and inspires each other to remain close although families live miles apart. The book's cover features James Arthur Call and Martha Wenzel Call on their wedding day, which was June 6, 1906.

On the 100th anniversary of Mother's Day, an article in a newspaper insert honored the creator of a special recipe. Although her mother had died several years earlier, and phone calls and notes had ceased, the author reconnected when she discovered her mother's recipe binder. It became a link to the past, as each recipe was like a conversation with her mother. "Looking at her script is like hearing her voice again," the author stated.[18]

One dessert, Grape-Nuts Pudding, was her favorite. The recipe instructions are like advice from mother. "Break the eggs and whisk them," the directions urged. The cook's hands become coated with ingredients and their movements mirror those of the mom. The recipes represent a continuing bond with her mother, who is greatly missed. "When I make this pudding, and all the other dishes she left behind, we are together in a way that is not a metaphor. A recipe is like a magic trick. It makes the past live."[19]

Many of us have failed to communicate family histories from one generation to the next. On numerous occasions I have heard people acknowledge lost opportunities. "If only my mother was here, she would know that answer," they will say. I can identify with them, as I have made the same comment on several occasions. Questions seem to come easier when the answers are no longer available. Once in a while, though, a nugget of family information will come to light.

My grandmother lived into her eighty-fifth year, when she died just two months after my grandfather. While he had died suddenly, her health steadily declined over those last two months that she spent without my grandfather. Many family members visited and were able to talk with her, as she was still alert and responding most of the time. On one occasion she told me about her oldest brother, Frank, who had served as a soldier during World War I. He had been shot and captured by the Germans, but they took care of him when they discovered that he could speak the German language. That was a piece of family history I had never heard from anyone before.

"Who's been holding out on us?" I thought, as I wondered how many other family details were never shared. From time to time I have pondered what interesting family histories might exist, but remain elusive for lack of specific conversations. When my mother died seven years ago, it occurred to me that I had never had those discussions with her. I had squandered an opportunity to learn a wealth of information about my family.

A focus on family history will assure that genealogical information is shared to maintain a continuity of awareness regarding ancestors. An effective practice is to conduct conversations during family meetings and holiday gatherings in order to share histories, verbal stories, and humorous events. A genealogy chart is a good start and a sample is included in Appendix E.[20]

Traditions

Since I spent a lot of time with my friend, Louie, as we were growing up, I was often at his house during the Christmas season. Each year I enjoyed the tradition of tamales, rice, and beans. They were accompanied by Christmas decorations and holiday music. Louie's parents, Louis and Catarina, hosted close friends in their furnished basement at that special time of year.

My good friend, Jon, quickly remembered the holiday gatherings at the Urdiales house during a recent conversation. Although that was 40 years ago, the memories come quickly rushing back during the holidays. I often eat tamales during the Christmas season and remember Louis and Catarina, but it will never be quite the same without them. They passed away several years ago and I miss them very much. They were like a second set of parents and the tradition of hosting friends during Christmas was a special legacy I will always cherish.

My sister, Linda, moved to the south almost thirty years ago to accept a teaching position in Aiken, South Carolina. Within a few years, she met Jonny and they were soon married. One of the traditions at the house of her in-laws, Mackie and Frieda, was a prayer at mealtime with everyone holding hands around the table. While we are Catholics like them, we had never held hands during prayer and, in all honesty, we had only prayed at special occasion meals with large family gatherings. However, I was inspired by Mackie and Frieda.

At some point I decided that our family should pray while holding hands at mealtime in our house. The tradition caught on very quickly with our grandsons, who now insist that we hold hands to pray before the evening meal. A simple practice of holding hands brings our family together and assures that we say a prayer. It is also a wonderful way to connect with guests in our house at mealtime. Our mealtime prayer has become a legacy of

Mackie and Frieda, who may be proud to know that they have influenced Yankees from Ohio with a favorable legacy.

You might consider communicating family traditions that you identify as important, such as events connected with holiday gatherings, and make certain they are shared with family members. If you do not currently have family traditions, this may be the time to develop them. It may be as simple as events tied to holidays or birthdays.

Messages to Others

The consideration of a legacy often leads us to develop messages for others, perhaps overdue conversations. However, too often people wait for "the right timing" as if a deathbed talk is a certainty, but that only seems to happen in the movies. The reality is that most people die without a chance to say good-bye and miss the opportunity to have one last conversation.

One of my new goals at my 50th birthday was to write a eulogy for each of my closest friends. I delivered it to them and welcomed them to either read it or save it until they are ready. The eulogy represents a statement I plan to deliver at each of their funerals, customized for each friend. By giving it to them in advance, they have a chance to read what I will deliver in case they go before me. It also provides my presentation which would have been delivered, but won't be given, if I go first. Either way, I have communicated my intention to honor their legacies and they can know in advance what I have to say.

We are all too good at making excuses and postponing action. If we simply wait to communicate at a later time, the day will never come and messages will go undelivered. Since it is unlikely there will ever be a "right time" or a "best time", it is necessary to choose "the time" to communicate messages that you want delivered. Only in western movies do the heroes hang on just long enough to "say their last piece." Each of us should reflect on conversations which have been put off and make a point to have them.

My wife and I have begun to schedule lunch visits with relatives and friends. We can never know when we might have lost a last opportunity to visit with those who are close to us and we never know when we might have experienced a lasting impression from them until it is too late. If we do not plan our visits, we will see family members only at funerals.

Revisiting Washington, DC

As I was concluding the writing of "Determining Your Legacy", I realized I had to bring closure to the main focus of my inspiration. I needed to travel to Washington, DC in an effort to reconnect with the National Park Service employee who first influenced my focus on lasting impressions with his generous request to "give a dollar to a homeless person whenever I see him."

I booked a flight into Reagan National Airport, printed turn-by-turn directions to the hotel, and reviewed a map of monuments on the National Mall. "I'd like to get a picture with the Park Service employee," I thought during the flight.

I was fortunate to quickly find a taxi at the airport and the driver eventually found the hotel. Once I checked in, I saw that my hotel was only a short walk from the major sights. In a matter of minutes, I stood among the monuments. Unlike most people there, my focus was not on the sites. My mission was to locate a specific person who had inspired me.

My search led me to scour the area surrounding the Vietnam Veterans Memorial Wall, but without success. Near the Lincoln Memorial I spotted an employee in uniform. I waited until she had completed her discussion with a small group and answered their questions. I then walked forward to inquire about the employee I first met nine years earlier.

"I would like to ask if you can help me. I am here to try to locate a National Park Service employee. He was working near the Korean War Veterans Memorial in the spring of 2004 and led me to the World War II Memorial. He is black, fairly thin, and more than six feet tall. When I offered him a tip or a drink, he refused to accept."

"I'm glad you had a good experience with one of our workers, but I really don't know who that would be," the woman named Jenna replied, "I have not been working here very long. However, there are several coworkers who have been working this assignment for many years. One of them should be able to help you. They are stationed at the Survey Lodge Park Ranger Station near the Washington Monument. You should be able to find the park employee there."

"Thank you very much," I replied. Jenna had given me a map and marked the location of the station, so I set off along the Reflecting Pool toward the Washington Monument. As I passed the World War II Memorial, I recalled the day I was led there by the kind Park Service employee. I saw the same concession stand where nine years earlier he had refused my offer of a cold drink or a tip for his efforts as my guide to the World War II Memorial. I also recalled the day he inspired me to begin my focus on lasting impressions. I was so thrilled that I was about to reconnect with the same Park Service employee who had impacted me with his legacy in 2004.

Have you considered your legacy for family members?

[1] Samuel A. Bent, *Familiar Short Sayings of Great Men* (Boston: Ticknor and Company, 1887), 42.

[2] Liz McCarthy, (Senior Vice President and Head of Corporate Communications), "*Parallels*", New York Life Insurance Company, aired Dec. 22, 2012, Television Commercial.

[3] Stephen Schwartz, Kristin Chenowith, and Idina Menzel, "Wicked: A New Musical", CD, Decca Broadway, 2003.

[4] Gerald F. Kreyche, "How to Make a 'Last'-ing Impression," *USA Today Magazine* 129, no. 2658 (2000): 82.

[5] Jim Rohn, "The Importance of Leaving a Legacy," accessed April 14, 2013, http://www.jimrohn. com/index.php?main_page=page&id=1294.

[6] United States Conference of Catholic Bishops, *The New American Bible* (Washington: United States Conference of Catholic Bishops, 2002), 1276.

[7] Stephen R. Covey, *First Things First* (New York: Free Press, 1994), 45.

[8] Merriam-Webster, "Merriam-Webster.com, " accessed Dec. 27, 2012, http://www.merriam-webster.com/dictionary/legacy.

[9] Alexa Ispas, "This Question Can Save Your Life," last modified June 16, 2010, http://www. alexaispas.com.

[10] Alexa Ispas, "Creating Legacy Manifesto," last modified June 9, 2010, http://www.alexaispas. com/creating-legacy-manifesto.

[11] Gerald F. Kreyche, "How to Make a 'Last'-ing Impression," *USA Today Magazine* 129, no. 2658 (2000): 82.

[12] Lorne Greene, "Mirror of a Man," *Bonanza,* directed by Lewis Allen and written by A.I. Bezzerides, NBC, aired March 31, 1963, Television.

[13] Samuel A. Bent, *Familiar Short Sayings of Great Men* (Boston: Ticknor and Company, 1887): 42.

[14] Dave Ramsey, *The Total Money Makeover* (Nashville, TN: Thomas Nelson, Inc., 2003), 62.

[15] Roger Allers and Rob Minkoff, (Directors), "*The Lion King",* recorded 1994. Disney, DVD.

[16] Gerald F. Kreyche, "How to Make a 'Last'-ing Impression," *USA Today Magazine* 129, no. 2658 (2000): 82.

[17] David F. Sutton, "A Tale of Easter Ovens: Food and Collective Memories," *Social Research* 75 (2008): 157-180.

[18] Sarah DiGregorio, "The Miracle in My Mother's Pudding," *Parade Magazine* (May 11, 2014): 8.

[19] Ibid, p. 8.

[20] "Free Family Tree PDF Charts," accessed April 14, 2013, http://www.misbach. org/freecharts/kids-chart.html.

Chapter 12
Planning Your Professional Legacy

"The gifted man bears his gifts into the world, not for his own benefit, but for the people among whom he is placed."
                                            – Henry Ford[1]

My inspiration for sharing the lasting impression story, the Park Service Employee, seems to reappear in the form of coworkers. Their conscientious effort often serves as an example for colleagues, a professional legacy.

One day I walked into the Atrium at the college and nearly stepped in a pile of nachos and cheese lying on the tile floor. My first reaction was to search for the student who had dropped the plate. I recalled watching episodes of CSI on television and I thought to myself, "I should be able to solve this mystery. There could be low velocity cheese splatter in the opposite direction of the culprit's escape. Maybe there is a footprint on the floor made by a unique size and style of shoe, but that was not the case."

Seeing no suspects nearby, my next thought was to call for a custodian with a mop before someone tracked the spilled cheese into an even bigger mess. The switchboard operator had hardly replaced the telephone receiver, when Sandy arrived to clean the floor. I expected to see frustration and to hear a complaint from the custodian, as I knew that would have been my reaction. However, she didn't frown for a moment or even hesitate with the mop, but quickly scooped up the mess and washed the spot. Her only comment was, "I just hope whoever dropped this plate had enough money to buy another one."

She was genuinely concerned for the student whom she was certain had accidentally caused the mess and Sandy worried about the need for the person to eat lunch. I felt guilty for my own reaction, in which placing blame on the perpetrator was my main focus. Sandy had left an impression on me of a truly conscientious employee and a compassionate person. She had quickly placed the needs of others before the effect on herself, which is a rare quality.

A Legacy of Quality Circles

I can recall others who also left a legacy, one of true professionalism. Beth, Frank, and Bob had each been hired during the same week in 1972 when the factory wage was $2.90 per hour for men and $2.75 an hour for women, a time when it was common for compensation to vary by gender. Workers punched a timecard by 7:00 am to start the workday and couldn't clock out until the eight-hour shift had ended at 3:30 pm.

Ten minutes of rest was granted each morning and again in the afternoon when employees were told to take their break. A thirty-minute unpaid lunch was allowed when a coworker could relieve each employee in sequence. However, workers in the Shipping Department could never enjoy a break in the cafeteria because the lunchroom was a fifteen-minute stroll from the warehouse. It was also impossible to return from a half-hour lunch without arriving late because of the thirty-minute round trip hike to the cafeteria.

Breaks and lunchtime were discouraging issues for Shipping Department workers who felt disadvantaged compared with employees closer to the cafeteria. Warehouse supervisors were constantly cranky because employees always returned late to their work stations. Like all of the shipping workers, Beth, Frank, and Bob dejectedly "put in their time" day after day from 7:00 am to 3:30 pm. Downtime was high and morale was low.

In 1982 the company adopted a new philosophy in the warehouse called "Quality Circles", a participative management practice which invited employees to contribute toward the identification, analysis, and solution of problems in their work.[2] Shipping Department workers were encouraged to attend training in the Quality Circles technique on company time, so Beth, Frank, and Bob stepped forward. Once they were trained, the three warehouse employees were requested to choose a project to develop a solution for a problematic issue. They quickly chose to design and build a break room in the warehouse. After eight months, a dozen meetings, and $48,000, an air conditioned mini-cafeteria was built in the Shipping Department. Workers could begin their break or start eating lunch after a few dozen paces instead of a fifteen-minute walk.

Proud of their success, the Quality Circle led by Beth, Frank, and Bob selected a second project to tackle. They realized that the employee locker room was just as far from the Shipping Department as the cafeteria. The Quality Circle was determined to plan and build a locker room beside their new break room in the warehouse. Fortunately for them, management was patient enough to support the Quality Circles effort and spent several thousand additional dollars on lockers for shipping department workers.

Within six months the warehouse workers were enjoying a new locker room and the recently completed break room. The third project of the Quality Circle team was a focus on loading trucks more efficiently. At that point Beth, Frank, and Bob were experienced at leading coworkers through the Quality Circle process. They quickly recruited key employees and encouraged them to identify weaknesses in the procedure for loading trucks.

Twelve weeks later the team presented managers their recommendations which ultimately saved the company $11,000 per month. While it appeared on the surface that the Quality Circles team had selfishly built themselves a break room and a locker room, their first two projects had reduced downtime during breaks and lunches by 300 hours per week. The problem solving experience gained during those first two projects prepared the Quality Circle team to rewrite work procedures, reducing the time it took to load trucks and increasing accuracy on the loading dock.

By valuing the involvement of employees such as Beth, Frank, and Bob, the company saw a surge in morale, productivity, and profit. "The more that responsibility can be delegated to others, provided that recognition is given for their achievements, the greater will be their respect and loyalty."[3] The legacy of the Quality Circles experiment is a memory of professional trust in employees and the success that they accomplished through the leadership of a creative manager who is fondly remembered.

The Value of Work

You will surely identify examples of your own parents with my memories. It was fun for me to snoop around the half-lit lobby at the grain elevator on Saturdays and inhale the sweet smell of animal feed with a molasses additive. As the manager, my dad had paperwork to finish, while I had rooms to explore. Later on, I witnessed my dad maintain a home office as a feed salesman.

Perhaps your mother also had a career. The family egg business was my mom's primary occupation. That enterprise required a daily commitment to feed chickens twice each day and gather all 13,000 eggs daily, often in hot, dusty conditions. Work has a way of paying the bills.

The summer after my part-time job in the grocery store, my parents encouraged me to apply for work at the tomato cannery in New Bavaria, a small town about three and one-half miles from my house in the country. The work wasn't too strenuous and it was a chance to make a few dollars each week.

I invested some of my earnings in a small Honda. The motorcycle was more fun than riding my bicycle seven miles round trip for the daily journey to work. I enjoyed the motorized commute for the last eight weeks of the summer. At the end of the season, I shook hands with Mr. Vanderhorst. I thanked him for the job and mounted my motorcycle. Midway through the trip, I slowed to turn onto a side road and the back tire slid on the loose stones in the intersection. The rear of the bike skidded across the road and I found myself lying on the pavement. Fortunately, I had not been traveling very fast so I just picked myself up and then the bike as well. I gained a positive impression from earning money at my part-time job that summer, but realized a negative outlook toward the bike. My last day of work that summer was also the last day I ever rode a motorcycle. Work teaches valuable lessons.

Like most college students, I held various summer jobs. Nine months of study followed by three months of work was a perfect transition. I was tired of studying after nine months of classes, but glad to return after three months of hard work. Summer jobs impressed me long enough to earn money for college. By the following spring, my empty bank account chased me back to the summer job market once again. Work and college complemented each other nicely as effective incentives. Work helps to discern the difference between a job and a career.

My grandfather was truly impressed when I completed a summer of work on the B & O Railroad. He had spent an entire career on the railroad and understood exactly what it meant to work on a "tie gang." I endured a long hot summer with dozens of workers and several machines which cut old railroad ties from the rails, pushed them out, inserted new ties, and spiked them to the rails. It took a lot of human labor to throw those remaining tie chunks, iron plates, and spikes off to the side. More machines then replaced the stones to hold down the ties and realign the rails. At the end of the procession was yours truly, who went into action when a plate had been mistakenly lodged under the track. My task was to jack up the rail, straighten the plate, and then swing the maul to spike it down onto the tie. My grandfather was so proud of my work that summer that he gave me a crisp, new ten-dollar bill. Work is a source of pride.

I was fortunate to have positive role models, so that working seemed like the normal thing to do. Once I was employed at part-time jobs, coworkers demonstrated guidelines for a positive work ethic. Later on, the influence of mentors provided positive role models of success.

Importance of Mentors

Early in a career, we are focused on landing a job, keeping the position, and performing well enough to be noticed for a raise. We define ourselves by a career in which compensation provides income to meet personal and family responsibilities. If each of us contemplates our personal situation, most of us will realize that we are the end product of others who have molded and improved the direction of our lives. It is good for us to acknowledge their effect on us, especially if we can thank them while they are still alive.

My friend, Dave, recently reflected on people who influenced him early in his career. Although it had been several years ago, their instruction had provided the encouragement for his successful electrical occupation. I found his way of describing them to be very interesting and insightful as he remembered coworkers.

"You don't notice at the time how a person impacts you, but I realized later in life that he was my mentor," Dave stated. "I really need to see Gordy and thank him before he cashes in his coupons."

At age 50, my friend George left corporate America. He had caught the bug of teaching while the Director of Training and a consultant to Fortune 500 companies and U.S. government agencies. George later taught management courses and mentored an entire generation of graduate and undergraduate students as a full-time professor at Harding University for 30 years.

One of Professor Oliver's most rewarding legacies is a student who attended class religiously and participated in class discussion, but could not succeed at written exams. After failing most tests during the semester, the student was fearful that he might fail the final exam. When he explained his dilemma to Mr. Oliver, the professor suggested an oral exam. He warned the student that the verbal test would be more rigorous and more comprehensive than the written test, but the relieved student was appreciative anyway.

After a 3 ½ hour intensive oral exam, Mr. Oliver was certain that the student had outperformed all of his classmates. The student passed the course, graduated, and became a very successful businessman. George Oliver's legacy is his inspirational mentoring of hundreds of successful business professionals.

Once we recognize the helpful influence of colleagues and mentors, we realize that our lives similarly represent a legacy for those who follow us. We provide a motivation for clients and coworkers which becomes our lasting impression, so we should strive to perform well when serving customers and inspiring colleagues. The real legacy is not recognition in the sense of honors, but a genuine legacy is our contribution to the profession and to coworkers who benefit from our example. Our true professional legacy is how we inspire others around us.

Servant Leadership

As Dean of Business, I tried to focus on the importance of people in my division. Over time I had discovered that every success is achieved through people. My true epiphany occurred during a business flight to Kansas City. I got a seat upgrade, extra legroom, and headphones so I could listen to soft music. A perfect trip led me to reflect on the value of a positive environment.

Although I had studied Maslow's hierarchy of needs like every student who has ever completed a psychology course, I did not take it to heart. I had grown up in the "old school", in which you were expected to work hard no matter how you were feeling. Instead of a focus on personal needs, the philosophy was "suck it up and work hard." However, during that special trip I happened to read the Marriott book "The Spirit to Serve". I was intrigued by the Marriott core value which focused on people first – "Take care of Marriott people and they will take care of Marriott guests."[4] I decided it was worth a try, so upon returning to campus I invited faculty and staff in the Business Division to let me know what I could do for them.

"I have become a disciple of Maslow, so please let me know how I can help meet your needs," I explained at a meeting.

One colleague suggested better coffee. "You know our coffee is chosen on least cost, and it tastes like it," she explained. I occasionally provided premium coffee from my wallet.

Another instructor asked if I could buy an ink cartridge for her printer. The machine had been purchased personally by her, so the college did not service it. "I can do that," I replied.

There was a colleague who did not drink coffee, but asked if we could have Mountain Dew sometimes in the kitchenette. I put a carton in the refrigerator once in a while.

I personally visited each faculty member to ask if there was something I could do to help them. At the start of the following academic year, I reminded everyone in the division that my role was to provide them what they need to perform their jobs.

"Please let me know how I can help you," was the reminder I sent them to begin the new academic year.

Six instructors responded with a similar email the same day. "Your offer works both ways," was the reply. "Please let me know how I can help you." I was blessed by the lesson to focus on needs of others, which was repaid by them with interest. The legacy of attention to coworkers is their motivation to serve the students.

A Legacy of Encouragement

Three decades ago Dr. Miller created the Faculty/Staff Development Fund at Northwest State Community College. He had many innovative ideas during his leadership of the campus, but none was more significant than the financial support of staff members in their pursuit of advanced degrees.

Over the years many faculty members and administrators have completed master's and doctoral degrees. Others broadened their understanding of educational administration, preparing them to be promoted into leadership roles. The legacy of Dr. Miller is the encouragement of personnel to develop their skills and the motivation to reach their greatest personal potential.

Leading with Respect

Bob Chapman became the CEO of HayssenSandiacre when the company was struggling. The first order of business was to meet with each employee to learn about his new company. What he found was a culture of distrust where employees dreaded going to work. Additionally, workers on the factory floor were treated much differently than office employees.

"Chapman understood that to earn the trust of people, the leaders of an organization must first treat them like people."[5] He told the head of personnel to remove timeclocks and pay phones. Locks were taken off of the parts cages in the maintenance department. Trust became the standard of the day and all employees were treated equally. The organization quickly felt more like a family. Workers took better care of machinery, reducing the number of breakdowns and the amount of downtime. Maintenance costs declined and productivity improved.

Success was not financed by debt, nor was it the result of reorganization. Assembly was not transferred overseas. No mass layoffs occurred. Business grew through efforts of the very same people who had worked there all along. They became committed to their employer because they felt valued. "Management gets results through people – to be competitive it is necessary to galvanise the resources of the entire workforce."[6] The company thrived and annual revenue rose from $55 million to $95 million.

"This is what happens when the leaders of an organization listen to the people who work there. Working with a sense of obligation is replaced by working with a sense of pride."[7] However, Bob Chapman's true epiphany occurred during a wedding ceremony where he watched the father of the bride hand his little girl to her future husband. It occurred to him that a groom accepting responsibility to protect his new bride is the same as a company hiring someone's son or daughter. "This is what it means to be a leader. Being a leader is like being a parent, and the company is like a new family to join".[8] The legacy of Bob Chapman is a lesson in the art of inspiring people to succeed.

Honesty and Integrity

Bill Pollard, former CEO and Chairman of the Board of The ServiceMaster Company, explained the importance of fulfilling commitments to customers and employees in his book, "The Soul of the Firm." "We must be people of integrity seeking to do that which is right even when no one is looking and staying committed whether the test is adversity or prosperity."[9]

My friend, Charlie, shared with me the inspirational story of his father. Dr. Beem was a cardiologist and surgeon who was the Director of Research at a pharmaceutical company, where he led the development of the first prescription drug for hypertension. He was later hired by a competitor as Director of Research, and was involved with clinical studies impacting FTC and FDA approvals.

However, Dr. Beem came home early one afternoon and called a family meeting in the kitchen, where he announced that he

154

was resigning from his position. He explained to his children he could not authorize a drug that had faulty research and he was aware that no study supported claims which the company made. He decided it was better to quit his job to maintain his integrity as an honest man. He soon received a government appointment to be Director of the National Institutes of Health and the National Heart Institute, where his work led to development of the artificial heart.

The legacy of Dr. Beem is a focus on honesty and integrity. I thanked my friend, Charlie, for sharing his father's story. "We can all benefit from the example of a virtuous man," I explained. Each of us is certain to face ethical dilemmas during our careers and it sometimes requires a concerted effort to pass the test. We can all benefit from the legacy of professionalism taught by Dr. Beem.

True Commitment

I recently interviewed a friend who manages a cleaning company. He shared that a major issue in the industry is low pay, which discourages effort by employees. Lack of motivation also leads to a serious turnover problem. Josh then told me an amazing story of commitment.

The manager explained that some workers, like 62 year-old Sally, never call in sick, clean offices until they are spotless, and beam with a pleasant personality.

"The only employee better than Sally," Josh explained, "is her mother."

"Are you serious?" I asked.

"That's right," Josh continued. "Marge is 82 and works four hours each afternoon, cleaning a local office. It nearly killed her when she was off work with an injury last year."

"Marge phoned to report she had fallen while mopping the tile floor in the office lobby and the doctor determined that her kneecap was cracked," Josh explained.

"But I can still work," Marge had told the supervisor. "I've been practicing with one hand on my vacuum cleaner and the other on my walker." Marge had been determined to return to her job.

"That's a level of commitment I don't often get to see," Josh stated. "I have to admit, she inspired me to work a little harder."

The Addition Business

A friend recently sent me an insightful blog written by Seth Godin. If you serve soup to 1,000 customers each day, holding back a few beans from each person means you gain a savings and almost no one is going to notice. If you run a call center and hire operators who make a dollar less per hour and are less well trained, even less caring, the impact on each customer interaction will probably seem small and you have saved a lot of money. If you manufacture cars and you can replace a bolt with a slightly weaker one, very few drivers will notice. If you make 200,000 cars a year, that will be a significant savings.

However, you know the problem. Some people will notice that the portions of beans in the soup are a little skimpy. Some customers who call for help will be annoyed enough to switch to another company. And some drivers are going to die because of less sturdy cars.

When we add up lots of little compromises, we get to celebrate the big win. But overlooked are the unknown costs over time, the erosion in brand reputation, the loss in quality, the subtraction from something that took years to accumulate.

In a competitive environment, the key question is, "What would happen if we did a little better?" We can add just a little more service, just a little better quality, or even just a smile. Organizations that add just a little bit every day always defeat those that are in the subtraction business.

The Park Service Employee Is No Longer With Us

The perfect ending of my story would be a reunion with the same Park Service employee who inspired the "lasting impression" focus. I hoped to learn his name and thank him once again in person for his positive influence.

Not far from the World War II Memorial, I found the small building near the Washington Monument with a sign which read "Survey Lodge." Inside I quickly recognized the distinctive short-sleeve gray shirt and olive green trousers. The uniformed man diligently answered visitors' questions. As the people walked away from the counter, I approached the white male with gray hair on each side of a bald head wearing wire-rimmed glasses. I introduced myself and again recited my interest in finding a National Park Service worker. I explained, "When I talked with him in 2004, he was probably in his forty's. He is black, fairly thin, and more than six feet tall. He was very helpful in directing us toward the World War II Memorial. He is the inspiration for a book I am writing and it would be great if I could find him."

"That is a great testament of his willingness to help," the man replied, "Let's see, I recall several employees over the years who might fit that description. I just need to reflect for a few minutes."

"When I offered him a tip or a cold drink for his help, he refused to accept," I explained. "Instead, he told me to 'give a dollar for him to a homeless man whenever I see one.'"

The ranger squinted, his eyes revealing that he was deep in thought while he slowly tapped his lips with an index finger. "Let me think on this for a moment. Also, tell me about your book."

"Well, I call it Determining Your Legacy," I explained. "It begins with a focus on first impressions, how they are fast, accurate, and long lasting. There are lots of examples in the book to reinforce each concept. However, the focus changes to lasting impressions when it is apparent that the first impressions often involve deceit, which betrays their accuracy. People frequently use deception to trick observers."

"Isn't that true!" he exclaimed. "Just when you think you can read people, they are fooling you!"

The phone on the counter rang and the Park Service employee pointed to the telephone to signal that he had to answer it. "Don't go away," he requested as he raised the receiver to his ear. "I believe I can solve your search for the man who left the impression on you."

I could hardly wait to hear the park ranger's answer and to honor the source of such an inspiring legacy. I wanted to thank that Park Service employee for his influence on others.

"I know who the worker was that you encountered years ago," the park ranger stated. "However, he is no longer with us."

Have you taken the opportunity to share your professional legacy which benefits colleagues?

---

[1] Henry Ford, *Ford News*, July 1, 1922: 2.

[2] David Hutchins, *Quality Circles Handbook* (New York, NY: Nichols Publishing Company, 1985), 31.

[3] Ibid, p. 142.

[4] J. Willard Marriott and Kathi A. Brown, *The Spirit to Serve: Marriott's Way* (New York, NY: Harper Collins, 1997), xii.

[5] Simon Sinek, *Leaders Eat Last: Why Some Teams Pull Together and Others Don't* (New York, NY: Portfolio/Penguin, 2014), 11.

[6] David Hutchins, *Quality Circles Handbook* (New York, NY: Nichols Publishing Company, 1985), 39.

[7] Ibid., p. 12.

[8] Ibid., p. 17.

[9] C. William Pollard, *The Soul of the Firm* (Grand Rapids, MI: Zondervan Publishing House, 1996), 66.

Chapter 13
Planning Your Spiritual Legacy

"In the very act of giving right praise to God, we achieve an inner harmony." – Dietrich von Hildebrand[1]

After a short pause, the Park Service employee spoke into the phone, "No, the stairway in the monument is still closed. It will remain closed as long as you see scaffolding around it." As he hung up the receiver, the man turned back to me.

"You mean that park service worker is no longer with us?" I asked with surprise.

"Oh, I don't mean the park employee is dead," the worker replied. "The ranger you are trying to find no longer works here. His name is Thomas and he now works at another historic site. But, tell me, what is the message of your book?"

"Well, the book emphasizes genuine impressions formed over a long time and recommends forming your own lasting impression," I explained. "That then becomes the legacy you leave for others."

"I can really identify with that," he replied. "Each of us has a continuing spiritual connection with those who came before us and with those who follow us. We should all be aware of the impression we make on others, our spiritual footprint of sorts."

Flashback – A Spiritual Legacy

My new friend in Washington, also a compassionate Park Service worker, reminded me of people I have witnessed whose concern for others is truly spiritual. For several years my friend, Kirk, has been a leader in the Shalom Food Pantry at St. John's

United Church of Christ. He assists with acquisition of food, schedules volunteers, and manages the distribution of food items every Tuesday afternoon. Through Kirk's leadership, families in southern Henry County do not go hungry.

Kirk also leads the Shalom Christmas program to insure that families in need will be able to enjoy a Merry Christmas. The program assists sixty families with more than 150 children each year. It takes many hours to identify eligible families and to invite them to participate. Each household receives a variety of food items for a complete Christmas dinner, along with gloves, hats, and three presents for each child ages sixteen and younger. Kirk catalogs the ages, genders, sizes, and preferences of all those children by creating paper tags. Volunteers select a tag, purchase and wrap the item as a gift, and deliver it to the church.

Kirk's leadership insures that each child will receive pants, a shirt, and an entertainment item. He coordinates participation from church members in many area denominations which assist in the Shalom Christmas. The effort is such a great project that three Catholic parishes and several Lutheran churches also assist.

By participating in such a worthy program, we are not only helping others, but teaching new generations the importance of charity. Even if we cannot afford much of a gift, in the words of Nathaniel Hawthorne, "generosity consists not in the sum given, but in the manner in which it is bestowed."[2] We are all encouraged to help others. In 1806 Thomas Jefferson wrote "I deem it the duty of every man to devote a certain portion of his income for charitable purposes."[3] The Bible promises that those who give to the poor will suffer no want (from Proverbs 28:27).[4]

As a leader in Shalom food distribution, and the annual Shalom Christmas project, Kirk assures a successful ministry which serves needy households. The generosity of time demonstrated by Kirk is only outdone by the graceful way in which he greets participants in the Shalom project. Each family member is treated with warmth and respect by his engaging style. Helpers are thanked and truly appreciated for their assistance. Kirk's legacy is a contagious concern for others, as his efforts inspire generosity in others and promote a spiritual legacy.

Spiritual Quotes

Some of the best quotes I have seen regarding service to others were summarized long ago. In his 1907 autobiography, Booker T. Washington stated "those who are happiest are those who do the most for others."[5] Emma Vernon, President of the West Virginia Graduate Nurses Association, told a conference in 1917, "As defined in an inscription over the doorway of a hospital in India, 'service is the rent we pay for a room on earth'."[6]

I am continually amazed how brief conversations present moments which cause us to stop and reflect on people who demonstrate good will. At a recent conference, I met a new attendee, Rajesh, from Gujarat, India. He was very attentive during the preconference training and appreciative of presenters.

During the conference banquet, Rajesh stood to serve salad dressing to each of us seated at the table. I jokingly told him, "If you do that well, the hotel will find you a waiter's jacket."

Rajesh replied, "In my religion, we believe that service to others is service to God."

Author Karen Armstrong explains the belief in God using everyday terms.[7] She states that the truth of religion can only be acquired by practicing, much like success in a game. "The rules of a board game sound obscure, unnecessarily complicated, and dull until you start to play, when everything falls into place."[8] In other words, participation is key to appreciating religion. It is not only an exercise of worship, but behavior which achieves inner peace.

If you are not already actively participating, you should investigate the reality of religion. This is not a "holier than thou" statement, but a recommendation to seek a moral compass, a religious person, someone you can talk with one-on-one such as a priest, minister, or spiritual advisor. A focus on spirituality leads us to focus on service to others, enhancing personal satisfaction as we increase the good will we spread to those around us.

The Case for Christianity

In his book "Mere Christianity", C. S. Lewis analyzes various philosophies, as well as lack of belief in religion.[9] He makes the case for Christianity and the case for theology in general:

"In a way I quite understand why some people are put off by Theology. I remember once when I had been giving a talk to the R.A.F., an old, hard-bitten officer got up and said, 'I've no use for all that stuff. But, mind you, I'm a religious man too. I *know* there's a God. I've *felt* Him out alone in the desert at night; the tremendous mystery. And that's just why I don't believe all your neat little dogmas and formulas about Him. To anyone who's met the real thing they all seem so petty and pedantic and unreal!"

"Now in a sense I quite agreed with that man. I think he had probably had a real experience of God in the desert. And when he turned from that experience to the Christian creeds, I think he really was turning from something real to something less real. In the same way, if a man has once looked at the Atlantic from the beach, and then goes and looks at a map of the Atlantic, he also will be turning from something real to something less real: turning from real waves to a bit of coloured paper. But here comes the point. The map is admittedly only coloured paper, but there are two things you have to remember about it. In the first place, it is based on what hundreds and thousands of people have found out by sailing the real Atlantic."

"In that way it has behind it masses of experience just as real as the one you could have from the beach; only, while yours would be a single isolated glimpse, the map fits all those differences together. In the second place, if you want to go anywhere, the map is absolutely necessary. As long as you are content with walks on the beach, your own glimpses are far more fun than looking at a map. But the map is going to be more use than walks on the beach if you want to get to America."

"Now, Theology is like the map. Merely learning and thinking about the Christian doctrines, if you stop there, is less real and less exciting than the sort of thing my friend got in the desert. Doctrines are not God: they are only a kind of map. But that map is based on the experience of hundreds of people who really were in touch with God – experiences compared with which any thrills or pious feelings you and I are likely to get on our own are very elementary and very confused."

"And secondly, if you want to get any further, you must use the map. You see, what happened to that man in the desert may have been real, and was certainly exciting, but nothing comes of it. It leads nowhere. There is nothing to do about it. In fact, that is just why a vague religion – all about feeling God in nature, and so on – is so attractive. It is all thrills and no work; like watching the waves from the beach. But you will not get to Newfoundland by studying the Atlantic that way, and you will not get eternal life by simply feeling the presence of God in flowers or music. In other words, theology is practical: especially now."[10]

Hopefully each of us will consider how we might be able to assist others in a manner which applies our time and talents to focus on the interests of people in need. With attention toward helping them, we will realize an increase in personal satisfaction and an enhanced sense of purpose in our lives. You will also find that others will learn from your example of concern. Your legacy will be a positive impression of service, generosity, and an inspiration to others.

If you are not currently participating in a religion, ask yourself a few quick questions:

1. Are you 100% sure there is no God?
2. Do you comprehend eternity in case you are wrong?
3. Are you prepared to be responsible if you lead others astray?

The question of religion is one which will not be answered completely, so it is not worth waiting for a definitive outcome. It is unlikely there will be a bolt of lightning or a booming voice from the clouds. That is why it is called faith.

Contagious Charity

In 2002 Chip Paillex and his four year-old daughter planted a garden and donated a surplus of 120 pounds of produce to a local food pantry. His effort grew each year into an organization of 4,000 volunteers who have donated more than 3.7 million pounds of produce in a period of 13 years.[11] Corporations and individuals continue to join the growing movement called "America's Grow a Row" to help those who are food insecure.

In September of 2014, Chip Paillex was named a CNN Hero. "CNN Heroes is a Peabody Award winning and Emmy nominated year-long initiative that honors everyday people for their selfless, creative efforts to help others."[12] Chip's organization truly extends a charitable solution to the hungry. They also provide an opportunity for volunteers to participate as charitable members of society.

I witnessed an opportunity to help others when I recently attended the annual conference of the Accreditation Council for Business Schools and Programs (ACBSP) in Baltimore, Maryland. As our group walked back to the hotel after dinner at a nearby restaurant, a shabbily dressed man asked if I could help him with a donation for food. Remembering that generous Park Service employee in Washington, DC, I reached into my pocket and then placed a few dollars into his hat.

Obviously appreciative, he said, "Thank you, my family thanks you, and God bless you!"

As the man walked away, my friend, Charlie, remarked, "That is a very generous gesture. The man is fortunate you were here."

"Well, Charlie," I replied, "I am also fortunate he was here. He provided me an opportunity to be helpful."

Not twenty feet later, another man stopped me for assistance. "Can you give me some money?" he asked, "I don't have enough to pay the fee to get my car out of the parking garage and my cell phone is dead."

I stopped long enough to respond, "You have a car and a cell phone? I won't give you money, but can I phone someone for you?"

"No thanks," the man replied, and slowly walked away.

The following day a colleague at the conference told me, "I saw what you did last night and that was a very good thing."

"Do you mean my encounter with the first man or the second?" I asked.

The colleague chuckled as he replied, "Actually, I saw both situations. While the first was a chance to perform a good deed, the second was a lesson for a less than needy individual."

When I saw a local opportunity to help a poor family, I was very proud of my grandson's explanation of a donation. We saw a young man holding a cardboard sign which read "Homeless with a Family" while driving past Wal-Mart. I turned the car around to drive back and then handed my grandson some money. As we stopped next to the man with the sign, Breyer rolled down his window and passed the donation to the man.

"Merry Christmas!" Breyer told him.

"God bless you!" the man replied.

Our younger grandson, Karter, had watched the scene from the back seat. "If he's homeless, where does he sleep?" Karter asked.

"Well, he probably counts on people to help him each night," I answered.

"What's he going to do with the money?" Karter inquired.

"Well, not everyone has a job, or a place to live, or food to eat," Breyer explained. "He will probably use the money to buy food and, if enough people help him, he can buy some clothes. At Christmas time we should be generous to help people."

Sometimes children reveal that they really do comprehend. I was very pleased to see that Breyer "gets it" and that he understands the spirit of Christmas. When he communicated the lesson to Karter, I saw that sometimes children can learn better from each other than from adults.

It is inspiring that the Park Service worker in Washington has created a legacy of good will that is still multiplying through me and others to help people in need. If it were not for that one chance encounter in Washington, DC, I would not be conscious of the needs of those around me. Charity toward others is the lasting legacy of that generous Park Service employee.

My wife and I recently drove to the nearby Bob Evans restaurant for breakfast. I had been given four coupons which expired at the end of the week, so I knew at least one of them would provide a discount. Alice indicated she also had an electronic coupon on her cell phone.

Since we didn't need them, Alice visited four different tables in the restaurant to share a discount coupon with other diners. As we left the restaurant, I commented that we had done a good deed by giving away at least $20 in discounts.

"Actually, we gained from the good feeling of helping others," Alice replied. "It was also an opportunity for one lady to feel good, as I watched her pass the coupon along to a young couple."

I realized that Alice was exactly right. We had gained at least as much as the recipients of the coupons. It truly is better to give than to receive.

The Prodigal Son

Even if we have not always been on our best behavior, we can change our ways. The Bible story of the Prodigal Son is one which both comforts and inspires (from Luke 15:32).[13] The example of repentance and forgiveness serves to ease our conscience, realizing that each of us can hope for compassion and forgiveness just as the Prodigal Son was welcomed back home. There is hope for all of us to find the right path, even when we stray, if we feel genuine contrition. Most saints did not run the best race through life from starting gun to finish line.

Just as we hope for forgiveness of our weaknesses, the story of "The Prodigal Son" inspires us to forgive others who have offended us. If our failings deserve another chance, we should be prepared to extend the same courtesy. I am continually impressed that such a simple story can be so powerful.

Forgiveness

Most of us have done at least one thing during a lifetime which we regret. Although we may feel sorry, or even confess our sin, the guilt may continue to fester. The longer that situation persists, the more it can haunt us. I recently viewed a television program with a story of forgiveness on TNT called "APB with Troy Dunn." One of the stories focused on the effort of a young woman named Marishka, who wanted to find the man who had killed her father in a car accident several years earlier. Her goal was to communicate forgiveness.

After several tries, and painstaking effort, the man was located. He had served many years in prison, missing his daughter's graduation, her wedding day, and the births of her children. He had suffered a tormented life with tragedies after release from prison, including a divorce from his wife. The man was found in the hospital, having recently suffered a stroke. The man's ex-wife and daughter whispered in his ear to tell him that Marishka forgave him. His demeanor immediately became very calm and he died ten minutes later. Marishka had provided him peace of mind at the very end of his life.

The effect was best summarized by the program narrator, Troy Dunn. "Forgiveness is the most difficult thing that a person can give another person," he stated. "But when one person gives another person forgiveness, both of them are healed."[14] This story might persuade you, as it did me, to schedule a visit and talk with someone whom I had offended earlier in life.

Inspiring Young Legacies

We often assume that religious leaders and parents are the role models for children, but we may be surprised. I recently served as usher at Mass with three high school students who were extremely attentive and worked to correctly perform each duty. We folded the bulletins, greeted parish members, and set aside baskets in a ready position for the offertory. When it was time to take up the collection, they asked for a few quick instructions, and then performed flawlessly.

As I reflected afterward, I was very impressed with the students and their commitment. I have seen them participating in church on many occasions. However, I had difficulty mentally placing them with their parents, who must be less regular attenders. Although life expectancy tables would tell us that the parents are much closer to the finish line of life, they were less active participants than their daughters.

One of my students was especially insightful as we discussed Ash Wednesday. Austin summarized the effect by saying, "We were formed from dust and we will always have an impact on earth. When we return to dust, it will never go away. It is much like the effect of our lives on others will always have an impact."

It occurred to me that students often serve as excellent role models for adults. They will grow up quickly, graduate from high school, and leave the house to create their own lives and families as adults. However, their impression and their legacy to parents is a lasting lesson of faith. Adults should be aware that children sometimes serve as role models for parents.

A Spiritual Investment

As was highlighted in the Mitch Albom book, "The Five People You Meet in Heaven", all of our lives are interconnected. What really matters on earth are the decisions each of us make and how we impact others around us. "We are here to add what we can to, not to get what we can from, life," is the lesson from Sir William Osler, first Physician-in-Chief for Johns Hopkins Hospital and the man who established the first medical residencies to study actual hospital patients instead of merely classroom lectures.[15]

If a stranger invited you to invest two pennies toward a future return of a million dollars, wouldn't you jump at the opportunity? You wouldn't have to know the man. You wouldn't have to see the plan. You would realize that there is little to risk. You would take that leap of faith toward the hope of a future reward.

A minister once stated that preparation for heaven is no more strenuous than the two cent investment. A life of faith and good works does not require us to give up very much. It does not expect a huge investment of money. After all, what else were we doing with our time and money? Do you remember how you spent your money last month? Can you recall what you did with your time last week? They are likely gone with nothing to show for them.

The ironic point is that a life of faith doesn't require us to change who we are. You can become a more genuine version of yourself like the U.S. Army slogan, "Be all you can be."[16] If you are already living a good life, a focus on your future isn't even a detour. Your investment of effort to believe in God is like putting two pennies toward that later return if you only consider the future that awaits you. The return on investment is infinitely valuable.

The oldest among us may live to be 100 years old. However, imagine for a moment what it would be like to live for 200 years, 500 years, or 1,000 years. As incredible as it sounds, that is a fraction of what it means to live for eternity. Likewise, it is impossible to truly comprehend the extent of eternity in the wrong place if we fail to properly manage our time on earth.

Therefore, it is extremely foolish to overlook the investment opportunity to earn an eternity in heaven. You don't need to know the man. You don't have to totally understand the plan. There should be comfort in knowing that millions of others have been on board with the program for 2,000 years.

If not for yourself, consider the significance of the legacy you provide others. As a father or mother, you are the role model for sons and daughters. As an uncle, aunt, cousin, friend, or neighbor, you are the inspiration for others around you. Your work ethic and integrity also provide the standard for coworkers. You teach them how to work toward their futures. You inspire them to invest in their eternity, one way or the other. Even if you don't do it for yourself, shouldn't you take the leap of faith for them?

My friend, Dick Gaietto, stated the importance of our spirituality by saying, "I believe that time is not my possession. I have been granted time on this earth with the responsibility to be a good steward of my time."

This book is not a prescription to tell you how to live your legacy, but the inspiration for you to develop your own personal plan. By determining your legacy, you will decide how you can inspire others and you will identify the appropriate steps to take in order to implement your plan. The Legacy Plan in Appendix F will assist with your deliberations.

Our Individual Faith Journeys

Each of us is at a different stage on our individual faith journey and we are all traveling at different speeds in that quest. The most important step is the next one we take on the way home and actions speak louder than words. C.S. Lewis wrote:

> "Christians have often disputed as to whether what leads the Christian home is good actions or faith in Christ. I have no right really to speak on such a difficult question, but it does seem to me like asking which blade in a pair of scissors is most necessary."[17]

According to another author, religion is not just what people believe, but something they do.[18] Success comes with experience. "Like any skill, religion requires perseverance, hard work, and discipline. Some people will be better at it than others, some appallingly inept, and some will miss the point entirely. But those who do not apply themselves will get nowhere at all."[19]

It is worth reflecting on the lasting impression of religion in our lives. We all go to great lengths to participate in less important activities. There are logo hats, season tickets, and pilgrimages to far away stadiums to cheer for our favorite teams. We regularly arrive early and stay late to experience the full effect of ball games. However, do we invest as much time and commitment to our personal futures?

One of my realizations was to review my own behavior. I have always changed the oil in my car each 3,000 miles and I have an annual vision examination each year. However, I was not a regular visitor to the confessional. Once I saw things in perspective, it did not make sense to take care of my car and my eyes, but risk my soul. Things had to change.

Until the Fathers of Mercy mission, I did not appreciate the concept of "conversion." I had pictured a conversion as the successful encounter between a mission priest and jungle cannibals if he happened to catch them between meals. However, I learned a conversion experience is the renewal of faith, typically triggered by a specific event, what you might call an epiphany. For some of us, our individual faith journey develops over time. Others are jolted into action by a specific event.

One Man's Epiphany

"How do you like my car?" an elderly man asked as he strolled across the parking lot of the Shell Factory.

While his gait was smooth, the wrinkles on his cheeks betrayed his age as he drew nearer. The blue and gold cap with "Korea" embroidered on the front displayed his vintage. He carried an empty plastic bag as he walked from the pond where he had tossed pieces of bread to geese swimming quickly toward him from the paddle boats.

I really had not noticed the small Hyundai in the handicapped parking space, but it didn't appear to be anything special. After a second look as I walked beside it, the car still seemed insignificant.

"It's nothing fancy, but I only spent $4,800 for a car with 19,000 miles on it," the man continued. "That loud guy that you see on Ft. Myers television really gave me a good deal."

As he turned closer, I could see the crucifix hanging from his neck. "I've got a medal similar to yours," I stated, as I pulled out the St. Benedict crucifix which hangs on a cord around my neck.

The man held his medal closer for my inspection explaining, "I've worn this since I got home in 1953. I told the good Lord if he let me live at Chosin Reservoir, I'd never miss Mass again."

"Tell me about the Chosin Reservoir," I replied.

"I was 23 years old when 120,000 Chinese attacked our 1st marines in Korea at Chosin Reservoir," the elderly veteran explained. "We were outnumbered 12 to 1 in weather so cold the guns froze. For 17 days we fought our way out. Less than half of us survived; the rest were shot or frozen."

The howling wind was interrupted by rapid gunfire which jolted the soldier from a half sleep. Raising his rifle just in time, he pulled the trigger to cut down the enemy soldier who silently peeked over the embankment. Another followed, then a third, and he squeezed off a shot each time to knock them backward.

Shots pierced the air to his left and right as the two marines behind him repeatedly fought off attackers. They desperately aimed in each direction with deadly fire as the wave of Chinese came at them. The barrage of bullets was punctuated periodically by a bursting grenade. The small band of soldiers had valiantly fought off enemy attacks multiple times every night for the past two weeks. Each time their fierce resistance had barely prevailed, and once again an uneasy silence set in.

What remained of their company still held the hill at the end of the shooting. Unfortunately, the Chinese weren't the only enemy. A continuous gale tore at the soldiers with 50 mile per hour winds. Even the piles of dead bodies surrounding the make-shift shelter did not insulate them from -30 degree temperatures.

Sparse meals consisted of frozen bites of bread and meat which were thawed inside the mouth before chewing. The latrineby-consensus was a spot two feet west of the marine's left boot. As the sun cleared the hill to illuminate the scene, soldiers stirred to collect meager supplies for what they hoped was a trek to safety.

As they crept forward through the brush, a burst of gunfire forced the marines to hit the side of the frozen hill for what little cover it provided. Bullets whined through the air and cut into the icy ground beside the crouching soldiers. Each of the marines fired a burst of shots to answer the Chinese attack. When the skirmish ended, cautious soldiers resumed the treacherous journey. The column of marines labored to carry along their ammunition, wounded, and dead comrades.

Scrambling quickly a few yards at a time, the soldiers scurried from one rock to another. The path in front of them exploded time after time as the Chinese threw one last attack, but a company of American comrades had rushed up to join the weary soldiers. The reinforcements brought better weapons and their relentless fire repelled the attack just in time to rescue the survivors. When the smoke cleared, navy ships emerged through the haze with landing craft waiting at the beach. The marines were saved!

The elderly man introduced himself as Trevor. As I shook his hand, I realized I had met a true American hero. He survived the war, worked hard his entire career, and lived his faith. This sunny January day in Fort Myers had provided a spiritual legacy.

"That day I survived the Chosin Reservoir my spiritual journey began in a serious way," Trevor explained.

An Extra Kick at the End of the Race

As I enjoyed the Sochi Winter Olympics on television, it occurred to me that most endeavors in life include a special effort, a "kick", at the end of the race. Whether it is the giant slolam, hockey, or ice dancing, athletes nearing the end of the event focus their best effort at the conclusion. The same effect was true for most events during the summer Olympics.

There is a desire to freeze the time clock or create a favorable impression on judges during the final opportunity. In most cases athletes are competing in their only international venue, or their last hoorah, and the result will become their lasting impression, their legacy for others.

Especially as we grow older and near the finish line of life, we realize our mortality. Even if we have lived a good life, we may strive to improve our habits toward the end just in case our lasting impact can use a boost. We may harbor uncertainty about our efforts. An August 18, 1805 journal entry written by Meriwether Lewis as he sat among the Shoshones on the Continental Divide reveals his assessment of the first half of his life's journey. "This day I completed my thirty-first year," he began. "I reflected that I had as yet done but little, very little indeed, to further the happiness of the human race, or to advance the information of the succeeding generation."[20]

Although few people in history have demonstrated such bravery in facing the unknown, and very few have contributed more to the future of the United States, Lewis regretted that he had not done more for mankind. He vowed that in the future he would live for mankind as he had previously lived for himself.[21]

I was intrigued when I heard a similar comment on different occasions from two of my close friends. "I find myself concerned at this point in my life," they each explained during separate discussions. "I'm just not sure I am good enough to get into heaven."

"None of us knows exactly what it takes to get in," I replied. "I've been told that those who are most focused on the goal are also most aware of their faults."

According to Peter Kreeft, "Ironically, it's the best people who most readily recognize and admit their own shortcomings."[22] I recalled reading a quote on the topic from Alexander Maclaren, "The worst man is least troubled by his conscience."[23] Those who are concerned for the future, then, are most likely to prepare for it.

Lasting Legacy of a Compassionate Ranger

Two children walked into the room and the Park Service employee looked my direction as he walked to the lower counter. "Please, don't leave just yet," he told me as I backed away to give more room for incoming traffic.

"Can I help the two of you?" he asked them. Their mother then entered the room and announced, "They want to complete the Junior Ranger program."

"Well, here's the stamp for this stop," he told the kids. "It looks like this completes your books! Here are your badges." He handed each of them a plastic badge.

When the family had walked out, the ranger continued to reflect on my book. "As we get older, we consider our lasting impact on others," he stated. "We often encounter people only one time, but leave our mark on them. "Take that family, for example," the ranger pointed toward the door. "They will never come this way again, but I hope my impression is positive."

"That's true," I replied, "It's like a friend told me. Once people reach our age, and their parents are gone, they focus more thought on what their legacy might be."

The Park Service employee replied, "Once our parents are gone, we really do take life more seriously. My father has been gone for several years and my mother died two years ago. I really miss them because I have no wife or children."

After a moment in thought, he continued, "Young people are so frivolous, but that's okay. They deserve to enjoy their youth, and they can wait to become serious later. At my age I realize how fortunate I have been. They actually pay me to talk with people here each day and direct them to the monuments. I hope I am able to share a positive legacy with visitors."

I told him, "Well, I know you've had a positive impact on me. Thank you very much for your time and our conversation."

He replied, "Thank you for sharing thoughts on your book and I hope you find Thomas. By the way, my name is Lloyd."

"My name is Larry," I replied as we shook hands. "Here is my card. If my book is published, I hope to help my special intention, the Fathers of Mercy, with the proceeds."

He then wrote his contact information on a sticky note and handed it to me. "By the way," he continued, "you have summarized the main purpose we have in this life. You can't know how much your story resonates with me, as I have no living family members to inspire. The legacy that matters is not that I might be remembered by visitors I serve, or even to be revered by coworkers. The legacy that matters is my ability to inspire them."

We shook hands and I walked out the door. I didn't know at the time that our meeting would be my last conversation with Lloyd and that he was about to determine his legacy for others.

Do you realize that you provide a spiritual legacy for others?

---

[1] Dietrich von Hildebrand, *Liturgy and Personality: The Healing Power of Formal Prayer* (Manchester, NH: Sophia Institute Press, 1960).

[2] Richard Alan Krieger, *Civilization's Quotations: Life's Ideal* (New York: Algora Publishing, 2002), 177.

³ H. A. Washington (editor), *The Writings of Thomas Jefferson: Being His Autobiography, Correspondence, Reports, Messages, Addresses, and Other Writings, Official and Private* (Washington, DC: Taylor & Maury, 1854), 589.

⁴ United States Conference of Catholic Bishops, *The New American Bible* (Washington: United States Conference of Catholic Bishops, 2002), 660.

⁵ Booker T. Washington, *Up From Slavery: An Autobiography*, (New York: Doubleday, Page & Company, 1907), 66.

⁶ Katharine DeWitt, Assistant Editor, "Nursing News and Announcements," *The American Journal of Nursing* 18, no. 2 (1917): 167.

⁷ Karen Armstrong, *The Case for God* (New York: Random House, 2010).

⁸ Ibid., p. xii.

⁹ C.S. Lewis, *Mere Christianity* (New York: The MacMillan Company, 1952).

¹⁰ Ibid., p. 135.

¹¹ "How It All Started", accessed July 21, 2015, http://www.americasgrowarow.org/about/.

¹² "About CNN Heroes", accessed July 21, 2015, http://www.annenbergfoundation.org/node/50751.

¹³ United States Conference of Catholic Bishops, *The New American Bible* (Washington: United States Conference of Catholic Bishops, 2002), 1119.

¹⁴ Troy Dunn, (Narrator), "*APB with Troy Dunn – The Gift/Forgiven*", TNT, aired Jan. 17, 2014, Television.

¹⁵ Sir William Osler, *Aequanimitas* (Philadelphia: P. Blakiston's Sons & Company, 1904), 20.

¹⁶ Beth L. Bailey, *America's Army* (Cambridge, MA: Harvard University Press, 2009), 192.

¹⁷ C.S. Lewis, *Mere Christianity* (New York: The MacMillan Company, 1952), 129.

¹⁸ Karen Armstrong, *The Case for God* (New York: Random House, 2010).

¹⁹ Ibid., p. xiii.

²⁰ Stephen E. Ambrose, *Undaunted Courage: Meriwether Lewis, Thomas Jefferson, and the Opening of the American West* (New York: Simon & Schuster, 1997), 280.

²¹ Ibid.

²² Lee Strobel, *The Case for Faith* (Grand Rapids, MI: Zondervan, 2000), 44.

²³ Alexander Maclaren, A Year's Ministry, Volume 2 (London: Office of the Christian Commonwealth, 1884), 82.

Chapter 14
Summary of Lasting Impressions

"An unexamined life is not worth living."[1] – Socrates

My awareness of impressions has shown me that the happiest, most successful, and most peaceful people among us are committed to love of family, respect toward coworkers, and reverence for God. They are the ones whose grandchildren often visit, former employees quote, and fellow worshipers emulate.

Importance of family was instilled in the next generation through traditions and love. They took time to mentor colleagues, teaching another generation the value of professionalism by example and love. They assist others in need and comfort mourners who have lost a loved one. Their spirituality inspires others around them with compassion and love.

The appreciation for family, coworkers, and God has a cumulative effect. Those who emphasize family values tend to grow in professionalism and spirituality. A greater focus on professionalism will lead one to enhanced emphasis on family and spirituality. An increased participation in spirituality is likely to create greater engagement in family and one's profession. As we deepen our commitment to family, professionalism, or spirituality, we achieve greater engagement in all three areas of focus. The most fulfilling life exhibits wisdom of all three legacies.

We Don't Know What We've Got 'Til It's Gone

My friend, Rita, had eaten breakfast daily at a local restaurant and I joined her there for ten years. We sat in adjacent booths on opposite sides of the tables so we could talk. I learned that a conversation with Rita was a wonderful way to begin the day.

When Rita died, it was truly a loss for me. I had begun many workdays by sharing an inspirational conversation and, when she became seriously ill, I had hoped she would soon be able to return to the morning restaurant routine. When she passed away, I realized that it had been inevitable for her booth to remain empty.

I stopped to eat before going to the funeral home. As I stared at the empty booth across from me, I recalled conversations I had enjoyed with Rita. I could almost hear her calm, raspy voice as so many times when she shared her nuggets of wisdom.

"You won't find me here any longer, you know," she would have quietly stated. "But if you behave, you will see me again."

At that moment, I became aware that the background music was playing a Joni Mitchell song from the 1970's and I recognized the lyrics. It seemed so appropriate as I heard the line "you don't know what you've got 'til it's gone."[2] As I reflected on many years of valuable conversations, I realized that I had once again experienced one of life's events which would never be duplicated. Sadly, there are many times that we don't recognize what we've got until it's gone. A clearer perspective of hindsight allows us to appreciate what we might not have realized while we were living in the moment. These are occasions that teach us to recognize a memorable event and to avoid taking things for granted.

The Bridge Builder

A former president of the college was often insightful, with just the right inspirational message. Whether an occasion was cause to celebrate or an event to commemorate, Larry had just the right poem or story. My favorite example was when he recited the poem, "The Bridge Builder."[3]

Although he would not admit it, when Larry read the poem, he was communicating the true legacy of his life story as a focus on the interests of others. He was truly the bridge builder.

The Bridge Builder

An old man, going a lone highway,
Came, at the evening, cold and gray,
To a chasm, vast, and deep, and wide,
Through which was flowing a sullen tide.
The old man crossed in the twilight dim;
The sullen stream had no fear for him;
But he turned, when safe on the other side,
And built a bridge to span the tide.

"Old man," said a fellow pilgrim, near,
"You are wasting your strength with building here;
Your journey will end with the ending day;
You never again will pass this way;
You've crossed the chasm, deep and wide;
Why build you this bridge at evening tide?"

The builder lifted his old gray head;
"Good friend, in the path I have come," he said,
"There followeth after me today,
A youth whose feet must pass this way.
This chasm that has been as naught to me,
To that fair-haired youth may a pitfall be.
He, too, must cross in the twilight dim;
Good friend, I am building this bridge for him!"

Whether our legacy is a focus on family, profession, or spirituality, the effect is to help the next generation. If we are successful, we will build a bridge for others which helps them to navigate the pitfalls of life. Our legacy is an inspiration which benefits others.

The Ultimate Lasting Impression

The ultimate lasting impression is the one that is already on file with St. Peter when we arrive at the gates of our last test. As he was given the keys of the kingdom of heaven (from Matthew 16:19), St. Peter will make the final decision regarding our eternal destiny.[4] Tricks and embellishments which might have characterized selfish first impressions earlier in life are no longer effective. Deception is not an option in our last test and it will be too late to change whatever impression we have created. Our lasting imprint on life has already been formed, and that is the perception which accompanies us in death. We can only hope that our lasting impression will represent us in a favorable light when our eternal fate is being determined.

As I drove past St. Luke's Lutheran Church, a sign posed the question, "Who have you caused to go to Heaven?" I thought, "Now there's a test of your legacy! That question should cause us to reflect." The answer might lead us to reconsider if the value of our impression on others has been sufficiently meaningful or if we can do a better job of inspiring others.

Summary of Lasting Impressions

Our journey through life is a process of decisions based on our impressions. However, as our focus shifts toward the interest of others, we achieve a more genuine satisfaction. An emphasis on lasting impressions leads us to complete that journey of life with a conscience. Our awareness of legacies leads us to determine how we are remembered and the impact we have on others. As I reflect on my journey of writing "Determining Your Legacy", the project is best viewed through examples. The significance of lasting impressions is characterized by individual stories which summarize the main point of each chapter in the book.

First Impressions Summary – A Generous Little Boy

The process of forming impressions about others helps to categorize them as positive or negative. The faster we judge others, the quicker we can get on with our decisions and the ensuing behavior to either accompany them or avoid them. As related in an earlier discussion, the process of forming impressions becomes so effortless and so natural that it occurs without conscious thought when observing others.

I took our grandson Karter grocery shopping with me on one occasion and he wanted to ride the mechanical horse in the store. "Do you have some pennies?" he asked.

"Sure," I replied, as I handed Karter four pennies.

When the horse stopped moving, Karter got off the machine. He placed the remaining pennies on the edge of the horse.

"Do you want to ride again?" I asked, "You have three more pennies."

"No," he answered as he pointed to the coins that had been carefully positioned on the machine, "another little boy may want to ride the horse and he might not have any pennies."

I was truly impressed with the concern for others displayed by Karter, when it might be more natural to focus on himself. At only eight years of age, he rarely thought about himself and often considered the interests of others. Karter is happy and mischievous, spreading humor and smiles, but well focused on being helpful. Such is the impression of Karter.

Speed of Impressions Summary – The Magic of Disney

First impressions are characterized by a quick, temporary fixation on a "big splash" event which moves us such as the big paycheck of our first real job or the immediate attraction of a first love. Maybe we are impressed by a shiny new car with a modern stereo system and an opening in the roof. Our motivations early in life are characterized by possessions and events which satisfy our short-term desires and trigger a fast impression. Sometimes a most significant event truly is a quick inspiration.

A few years ago, a student in my internship class worked the fall semester as an assistant manager in one of the departments in the World of Disney Store at Disney Marketplace in Orlando, Florida. One of her reports explained assistance to help a customer select the right gift.

"I want to buy one of these character dolls, so can you help decide which I should get? It is for a child in the hospital who is terminally ill and I want to get it to her as soon as possible," the female customer explained.

"Just one moment, please," the student responded, "I would like to share your question with my manager."

The customer did not wait long, as the two workers quickly returned. The manager's decision was immediate. "Ma'am, you won't have to choose which figure to buy. We're giving you one of each character for that special child because this is Disney."

"I couldn't hold back the tears," the student wrote in her report. "I had witnessed how, in this place, dreams really do come true. I'm not surprised that Disney has a highly motivated staff, maintains a high rate of employee loyalty, is one of the recognized 'best companies to work for', and is one of the most admired employers in the country. During just the second full day of my internship, I was totally blown away by the quick impression of such a caring organization here at Disney. The customer had tears streaming down her cheeks as she hugged the manager."

When a company is true to its mission, the first and fastest impression will be positive. The organization which functions with a genuine purpose does not have to be concerned with creating an impression, as its normal operating procedure develops a favorable impression which is quickly perceived by others.

Accuracy of Impressions Summary – Home Town Quality

When we are experienced in life, we learn to respect advice from long-term friends and to rely upon local businesses with whom we have enjoyed years of experience. I recently "rediscovered" the local appliance store after buying several items from a national chain outlet. When I was disappointed with the sales person at the chain store, I decided to try the local shop.

Vince's TV & Appliance store actually had a lower price, provided better service, and employees were more personable. I was quick to recognize a more accurate impression of good service at the local store as well as a genuine desire to satisfy customers. Sometimes the best decision is closer than we realize. We just might not appreciate how accurate our earlier impression had been.

"How's that dishwasher running?" Dave asked several months later. He was genuinely focused on customer satisfaction, reinforcing my accurate impression of personal service.

Longevity of Impressions Summary – A Lunch Tradition

Later in life many of us realize the lasting impression emphasis of a long-term career which has successfully served us, just as we appreciate a dependable car which has delivered us to many destinations in comfort. We have also learned to value a life-long relationship with a spouse as a best friend forever. What impresses us is a loyal companion who has faithfully stuck with us through thick and thin.

My wife and I recently ate lunch at a restaurant known for great desserts. We noticed an elderly gentleman at the table beside us who was wearing a bright plaid sport coat and light blue trousers. He slowly shuffled his feet as he balanced a piece of chocolate cake on a small plate in one hand and gripped a wooden cane with the other.

"You've made a good choice," I commented as he stopped to set the plate on his table.

"Yes, and I have enjoyed this dessert each Sunday for many years," he replied as he slid into his chair. "I have dressed up in these same clothes and enjoyed this wonderful lunch after church each week. Until she died last year, this was the Sunday tradition for my wife and me."

After a pause, he continued, "She used to wait until I was almost finished and then steal the last bite of chocolate off my plate. After more than sixty years of marriage, she still played tricks on me. Now I continue to dress up, go to church, and return here each week for lunch. I still save the last bite of cake at the end of each meal to see if it might disappear off my plate."

At that moment the waitress stopped to refill the old man's coffee. "Last week I got excited when I returned from the restroom and the bite of cake was gone," he explained. "Then I saw it lying on the table. The server must have bumped my plate when she refilled my coffee."

The elderly man laid down his fork when he had almost finished the cake and sat back in his chair. As we told him goodbye, I noticed one last bite of chocolate on his plate. I will not forget the old man's dedication, his tradition that continues to celebrate the longevity of his love.

Positive Impressions Summary – Caring Across Cultures

Eventually we realize that our lives have been enriched and enlightened by others who came before us as supervisors, coworkers, parents, grandparents, friends, and neighbors who inspired us with their positive impressions. Those whom I have thanked for their inspiration, their leadership, their favorable impression on me, are surprised to hear my appreciation. They are unaware that their example has created an impression, that they have impacted others around them. In most cases it happened unintentionally just by their positive efforts.

Several years ago I had the good fortune to travel to Greece for a conference and my wife, Alice, was able to join me. We chose a sunny day to tour the Parthenon, then we walked down the hillside into Athens. We found a small street-side café and enjoyed a Greek salad at a table on the sidewalk with a perfect location to appreciate a view of the Acropolis.

While we finished lunch, a shabbily dressed man, obviously tired and overheated, walked up to the waitress and, after a few words, she motioned him to a nearby table. Once he sat down, the man was served water and coffee. I told Alice, "That's a wonderful gesture. Where else in the world would you see water and coffee given to a person in need?"

Two days later our friend, Kirk, provided us a ride from the airport. I told him I would be glad to buy dinner on the way home, so we stopped at a restaurant in Wauseon, Ohio. Shortly after we were seated, a poorly dressed elderly man walked in carrying Wal-Mart bags. He told the hostess he was hoping he could sit for a few minutes. He explained his walk on the way home had tired him and he just needed to rest. The server waived him to a nearby table, and then brought him water and coffee.

The elderly man turned and said, "Isn't that nice of her to give me coffee and a place to regain my strength after a long walk. I can't stay long, though, as my wife is waiting for me to return from shopping." I was truly amazed. Within two days I observed the same generosity in two different cultures separated by 5,000 miles. If we only take the time to notice, we will observe behavior around us which impacts the course of our futures, thereby creating a legacy of those whose example is a positive influence.

Negative Impressions Summary – A Deceptive Legacy

The First Impression focus is a short-term emphasis on selfish, immediate gratification goals which, once accomplished, do not later seem as satisfying as we had expected. When "living in the moment" does not make us happy, we crave a quick fix of income to buy more possessions, striving for greater satisfaction and social status. However, we remain miserable because our fascination with making money and buying things does not bring us true happiness. People often trash their values and ruin relationships in an obsession to buy happiness. However, the immediate gratification was not achieved because the happiness we anticipated was only an illusion. Our selfish personal philosophy is similar to the "do anything for profit" strategy implemented by some deceptive companies.

LifeLock, the identity theft protection company, was ordered to pay $12 million in a 2010 settlement of Federal Trade Commission charges and lawsuits filed by 35 states because the company misled consumers about the effectiveness of its service. LifeLock was ordered to refrain from making further deceptive claims and to implement measures to safeguard the personal information received from customers.[5]

Jon Leibowitz, FTC chairman, stated "while LifeLock promised consumers complete protection against all types of identity theft, in truth, the protection it actually provided left enough holes that you could drive a truck through it."[6] The commission also cited that the "fraud alerts" LifeLock placed on individuals' credit files protected against very limited identity theft, mainly the opening of new accounts, which include fewer than one in five cases of identity theft.

The biggest problem with the company's claims was its guarantee to prevent identity theft from happening, while nothing can be done to create a 100% guarantee. When LifeLock CEO

Todd Davis broadcast his social security number to demonstrate the company's foolproof security, a man in Texas successfully got a $500 payday loan using Mr. Davis's social security number.

When Lifelock failed to fulfill the terms of the 2010 settlement, the FTC ordered Lifelock to pay $100 million in 2015 to settle contempt charges as the largest enforcement penalty ever assessed by the FTC.[7] Consumers are disappointed when businesses fail to deliver what has been promised, and they can be truly unforgiving when they are purposely deceived.

False Impressions Summary – Have I Got a Deal For You

We are often disappointed by products and services which do not function as expected. While at times the consumer has simply made a wrong choice, there are occasions when others have taken advantage of them. When people purposely mislead us, there is no definitive clue that someone is being deceitful. "Only Pinocchio had an obvious signal that was present every time he was lying."[8] Unfortunately, there are times that we have been tricked by sellers or even misled into a "get rich quick scheme."

The man who led a successful investment firm on Wall Street was a previous chairman of the NASDAQ and served on the board of directors for many charities. Old friends as well as new acquaintances were impressed by his engaging charm. However, he committed the largest financial fraud in United States history.[9] Only $1 billion has been recovered of the $170 billion prosecutors want returned.[10]

Bernie Madoff was able to con strangers as well as longtime friends because his deception was so complete and continuous. Even a dear friend, and lover for many years, was swindled of her savings. Another close friend of fifty years had earlier declared him to be such a great person, but then had the financial rug pulled out from under him as well.[11]

Madoff had mastered the ability to manipulate others without remorse. Once he gained their trust, he controlled the ability to hide account balances and move money. The control of information allowed a deceptive presenter to regulate the type and amount of cues delivered to clients. While the reviewer typically has the advantage in observations, it certainly is not true when one of the parties employs deception.[12]

The scam eventually defrauded investors of billions of dollars, destroying the savings of charitable organizations, businesses, and families. Hundreds of elderly men and women saw their life savings disappear and their quality of life plummet, as they could no longer afford to keep their houses or even to put food on the table, a truly negative impression.

Genuine Impressions Summary – A Legacy Inspires a Legacy

While in our early years we may not have appreciated comments from others, we realize later in life that advice is really shared wisdom gleaned from their experiences. They now have our complete attention, as we approach the finish line of life, for we can use all the help we can get. We learn to appreciate those whose genuine impression is a legacy of helping others.

On September 11, 2001, Delta Flight 15 was told to land as quickly as possible. As all flights over the United States on that morning, the plane was grounded. The Atlanta-bound flight from Frankfurt, Germany landed at Gander, Newfoundland.[13] By the end of the day, 41 planes were directed to interrupt their transatlantic flights by landing at the same airport.

The thousands of passengers outnumbered the population near Gander. However, the generous hospitality of people comforted the unexpected visitors. The passengers from Delta Flight 15 were taken to the small town of Lewisporte, where residents provided shelter in churches, schools, and homes. The "plane people", as they were called, received every consideration of food, shelter, bedding, laundry, and medicine. They were hosted on tours of the island and attended various entertainment events during their stay.

Upon departing, the overwhelmed passengers planned a way to thank the people of Lewisporte during their flight to Atlanta. The outcome was an endowed Lewisporte Area Flight 15 Scholarship Fund. While passengers pledged more than $15,000 by the time the plane landed, the fund grew each year. By 2010 more than $1 million had been raised and annually at least 10 high school students receive a scholarship toward college or vocational/technical training. Each year the leader of the effort, Shirley Brooks-Jones, returns to Lewisporte to present the scholarships at the high school graduation ceremony.

While events of September 11, 2001 were tragic, one legacy is the friendship and generosity of the people of Lewisporte. Their hospitality will never be forgotten by passengers who were stranded in the midst of a crisis. The reciprocal legacy is the continuing thanks of stranded travelers, who endowed scholarships to benefit future students of the community which afforded them more kindness than could have been expected.

Lasting Impression As a Legacy – Two Piles of Dirt

Eventually we are impressed by efforts with long-term impact which are truly satisfying and engage other people. A focus on others benefits them and provides a continuing source of satisfaction when we realize that there is a genuine purpose in what we do. As we accomplish good works which are outwardly focused for the good of others rather than inwardly selfish, we are creating our impression on others. We finally realize that what really counts is how we interact with others, how our relationships as colleagues, as coworkers, with family members, and with friends are the lessons that truly matter in life. Those interactions with people define our lasting impression on others, our legacy.

A Gospel passage provides a valuable lesson for all of us regarding our lasting impression (from Luke 12: 13-21).[14] The story focuses on a wealthy man who has not realized the importance of lasting impressions or a focus on others. His main goal in life is the accumulation of possessions, but, when he dies prematurely, he never enjoys his wealth and he is judged on his failure to help others.

Father Cunningham's homily shared a story which reinforces the point. In his youth, he worked for a cemetery digging graves. On one occasion, there were two funerals on the same day. He and an older man prepared graves at two ends of the cemetery, one for a poor man and the other for a rich man. The poor man's gravesite had a simple, small awning with a few flowers where a handful of close relatives gathered for a short committal service. The wealthy man's graveside service included a huge tent where a long procession of limousines arrived, carrying men in expensive suits and women in lavish dresses. There were several bagpipe musicians and huge sprays of flowers, including elaborate bouquets.

When both services had concluded, mourners quickly left and the tents were removed. Once the graves had been filled, the older man asked his coworker, "What do you see now?"

A young Father Cunningham replied, "What do you mean?"

The man answered, "All you see now are two piles of dirt. In the end it doesn't matter if we were rich or poor, if our life was simple or important, we each end up with a pile of dirt."

Forty years later, the message is still vivid. It does not matter if we are rich or poor, famous or not, we all end up the same. What counts is not how much we have accumulated, but how we have spent our lives and whether we have lived for others as our lasting legacy.

Final Thoughts on Legacies

Father George explained to the audience, "The takeaway value of lasting impressions is appreciation for the true lessons of legacies. Loving your neighbor as yourself is wishing what is best for them, which means our attainment of Heaven.[15] When others volunteer advice, they are not passing judgment on us. Family, friends, and coworkers encourage us to fulfill what is in our best interest – to pay attention to the Bible, to follow the 'Golden Rule', and to demonstrate concern for others. Mentoring clarifies right from wrong, although many fail to appreciate advice which confronts one's freedom to choose. However, it would be far worse to overlook wrong behavior in the name of 'freedom of choice' than to exercise a teachable moment to communicate 'right behavior'. A true legacy provides helpful hints for our pursuit of Heaven."

"We benefit from frequent reminders," Father George continued, "just as each of us learns from consistent advice. Repetition in teaching is much like the advertising rule of seven: it takes seven times for a message to guarantee a sale.[16] We all benefit from lessons to stay on the right path, and it may take several examples for the message to clearly hit home. This is the lesson of 'Determining Your Legacy' as demonstrated by Dr. Zach and the one whose life we honor today."

When I heard Father George mention my name, I was jolted out of my daydreams and back to the memorial service. "Get your game face on," I thought to myself. "This is my moment."

Your legacy is a valuable impression for others!

[1] Plato, *The Apology of Socrates*, translated by D.F. Nevill (London: F.E. Robinson & Company, 1901), 77.

[2] Joni, Mitchell, *Big Yellow Taxi,* © 1970 by Reprise, RS 20906, Single.

[3] Will Allen Dromgoole, "The Bridge Builder," in *Father: An Anthology of Verse, eds.* Margery Doud and Cleo M. Parsley *(New York:* E.P. Dutton & Company, 1931), 86.

[4] United States Conference of Catholic Bishops, *The New American Bible* (Wichita, KS: Fireside Catholic Publishing, 2010), 1035.

[5] Edward Wyatt, "LifeLock Settles With F.T.C. Over Charges of Deception*,"* last modified March 9, 2010, http://www.nytimes.com/2010/03/10/business/10ftc.html.

[6] "LifeLock Will Pay $12 Million to Settle Charges by the FTC and 35 States That Identity Theft Prevention and Data Security Claims Were False," last modified March 9, 2010, http://www.ftc.gov/opa/2010/03/lifelock.shtm.

[7] "LifeLock to Pay $100 Million to Consumers to Settle FTC Charges it Violated 2010 Order," last modified December 17, 2015, https://www.ftc.gov/news-events/press-releases/2015/12/lifelock-pay-100-million-consumers-settle-ftc-charges-it-violated.

[8] Paul Ekman, *Emotions Revealed: Recognizing Faces and Feelings to Improve Communication and Emotional Life* (New York: Owl Books, Henry Holt and Company, LLC., 2003), 217.

[9] Chris Michaud, "Madoff Says He Is Happier in Prison Than Free," The New York Times, last modified Oct. 27, 2011, http://www.reuters.com/article/2011/10/27/us-madoff-interview-idUSTRE79Q56H20111027.

[10] Chad Bray and Amir Ef, "Madoff Pleads Guilty to Massive Fraud," The Wall Street Journal, March 11, 2013, http://www.theaustralian.com.au/business/breaking-news/madoff-jailed-after-pleading-guilty/story-e6frg90f-1111119119325.

[11] Lionel S. Lewis, "How Madoff Did It: Victims' Accounts," *Society* 48, no. 1 (2011): 75.

[12] Ibid., p. 70.

[13] Katherine Harben, "Where the Heart Finds a Home," The Ohio State University Alumni Association, last modified Jan. 21, 2010, http://www.ohiostatealumni.org/media/Pages/WheretheHeartFindsaHome.aspx.

[14] United States Conference of Catholic Bishops, *The New American Bible* (Washington: United States Conference of Catholic Bishops, 2002), 1115.

[15] Fr. George McInnis, *"Christ Our God, Truth Incarnate" DVD,* Fathers of Mercy, 2010.

[16] Tom Ahern, *Raising More Money With Your Newsletters Than You Ever Thought Possible* (Medfield, MA: Emerson & Church, 2005), 105.

Chapter 15
Lasting Impression Conclusion

"No kind action ever stops with itself. One kind action leads to another. The greatest work that kindness does to others is that it makes them kind themselves."[1] – Amelia Earhart

Father George announced to those assembled in the Chapel, "I will now ask Dr. Zach to step forward and join me. We invite you to say a few words."

It was only a few steps to the pulpit, as I had been seated with the celebrants near the altar. They had asked me to join them ahead of time as they prepared for the memorial service and Father David invited me to sit up front through the service since I would be a speaker.

As I walked to the microphone, my thoughts were drawn to the man who was the true focus of the memorial. I am not the source of the inspiration, but merely the messenger of his lasting impression.

The importance of people who inspire others has been recognized by many authors. Ralph Waldo Emerson believed "the true test of civilization is, not the census, nor the size of cities, nor the crops – no, but the kind of man the country turns out."[2] Author Mitch Albom advises "that there are no random acts. That we are all connected."[3]

The real test of a life well lived is whether we serve as an example to encourage others. If we can ignite a passion to help others, if we provide a powerful lasting impression, we will inspire the future. Peers, employees, and children are likely to follow your example, as the behavior you demonstrate can become contagious. Parents may determine the actions of sons and daughters, while effective managers often inspire effective employees.[4]

Lasting Impression Journey

Lessons in our life journey are all-encompassing, as each of us is somewhere between the first impression emphasis and the lasting impression reality. Our current focus depends on the individuals and events which have guided us. As my friend Charlie recently clarified for me, it is beneficial for us to be reminded of the people in our lives, as none of us completes the journey through life alone. Each of us has been influenced and we impact those around us in the same way that a domino tipping over within a chain reaction creates a series of cause and effect impressions which influence other people.

The focus on lasting impressions is a journey from a superficial quest for short-term goals to a genuine appreciation of long-term values. From "living in the moment" to "living a plan", from a selfish focus on "me" to a caring focus on "others", impressions evolve into a focus on the lasting impact toward others. While a First Impression Focus is a natural starting point in life, maturity leads us to the inevitable destination of the Lasting Impression Focus.

Hopefully memories of your own life experiences have been triggered by the examples in this book. There is much to be learned from a friend, neighbor, parent, aunt, uncle, or grandparent while they can still share an inspiration with us. Likewise, now is the time to reflect on the lasting impression which will persist among descendants long after we are gone from this life and to determine the legacy that we will pass along.

You represent the link between the past and the future. You can benefit coworkers by guiding them through mentoring as your legacy to them. Since none of us knows how long we will be alive

196

on this planet, we must act immediately or miss opportunities to both learn from others who precede us and to inspire those who follow. Your example can also serve to inspire others as your spiritual legacy. As Saint Basil stated, "A tree is known by its fruit; a man by his deeds. A good deed is never lost; he who sows courtesy reaps friendship, and he who plants kindness gathers love."[5]

With only one lifetime, only one career, we must carefully arrive at decisions which influence others. Many years ago, a dear friend introduced me to the music of Seals and Crofts. The most moving song for me is a message that we have to make the most of our time in this world. Since I may never see my friend again, the song that sticks with me is "We May Never Pass This Way Again."[6] The lyrics are a constant reminder to make the most of our one and only trip through this life.

The Memorial at the Chapel Concludes

After pausing for a moment to steady my voice, I was determined to speak clearly. "Thank you for your recognition, but it is I who thank you, Father David, Father George, Father Louis, and all of you at the Fathers of Mercy. Your missions inspire people everywhere to take up the cross in pursuit of salvation, each according to wherever they currently stand on their personal faith journey. Thank you for changing the lives of all you encounter with your lasting impression."

"I would also like to take this opportunity to recognize the inspirations of my focus on lasting impressions," I explained. "Thomas Black, an employee with the U.S. Park Service, refused a tip and the offer of a cold drink in Washington, DC, preferring to request that I focus on helping homeless people whenever I see them. His concern for people in need inspired me to write the book 'Determining Your Legacy'."

"When I traveled back to Washington nine years later to look for him, I met another park ranger who immediately connected with the legacy focus of lasting impressions," I stated. "That man is the person we honor with this memorial service. He quickly demonstrated his unselfish belief in assisting others around him. While he had no wife or children, he had created many lasting impressions as he helped all who encountered him. He was not wealthy in dollars, but he was rich in legacies that he had provided for others with his generous guidance at the Washington, DC monuments."

"He responded to my visit by sending me a generous donation for my special intention, which is the Fathers of Mercy," I explained. "Lloyd Cook is that donor."

I held up a small paper and continued, "This note that he attached to his check reads, 'I hope this donation will motivate others to be generous toward those in need. I would like that inspiration to be my personal lasting impression legacy for others'."

"I didn't know when I met him that Lloyd was terminally ill and had no family," I shared. "Three weeks later he died quietly in a small house in a Washington, DC suburb." After a pause, I continued, "Well, his effort is truly a lasting impression and deserving of this memorial."

"I ask you to help people whenever you see them." I explained, "When you help others in need, and especially when you influence other people to do the same, you are honoring the legacy of Lloyd Cook in a special way that he would most appreciate."

As my remarks ended, I peered beyond the pulpit to see the faces of my closest friends in the front pew, some of them wiping their eyes. The service concluded with a blessing from Father David to those assembled. Celebrants then gathered together for the recessional and this time I walked along, following the brothers who carried the cross and candles. The priests came after me, walking down the center aisle as they sang the closing hymn, toward the back of the Chapel. We all turned to the side to wait for people filing out after passing the last pew just as the music ended. I shook hands with the priests as each of them thanked me.

Participants stopped to greet the priests on their way out of the Chapel and some took a moment to shake hands with me. I felt so proud to be associated with the religious order as a friend of the priests and a benefactor of their inspirational work. As Alice and my close friends finally arrived at the back of the church, it was an occasion for hugs all around. By the time we stepped outside, I watched the small crowd of people talking with each other and smiling. It occurred to me that there were many who walked away with a renewed focus on their individual faith journeys, a positive influence from the memorial service, and a lasting impression as a legacy of the Fathers of Mercy and an inspirational Park Service employee. Although I never found Thomas Black, the original Park Service employee, Lloyd Cook had renewed the inspiration of a selfless man who only cared for others.

I caught up with Father George to thank him for providing a special influence of lasting impressions. He had previously shared an insight which demonstrates the stages of forming a legacy. As he puts it, "Every thought tends to become a desire, every desire tends to become an action, every action tends to become a habit, our habits define our character, and our character determines our destiny."[7]

Such is the power of a lasting impression and your ability to determine a legacy for others!

[1] David R. Hamilton, *Why Kindness Is Good for You*, (Carlsbad, CA: Hay House, Inc., 2010), 228.

[2] Ralph Waldo Emerson, "American Civilization," *The Atlantic Monthly* 9 (1862): 506.

[3] Mitch Albom, *The Five People You Meet in Heaven*, (New York: Hyperion, 2003), 48.

[4] Jack Zenger and Joseph Folkman, "The Trickle-Down Effect of Good (and Bad) Leadership", Harvard Business Review, last modified Jan. 14, 2016, https://hbr.org/2016/01/the-trickle-down-effect-of-good-and-bad-leadership.

[5] Marlene Caroselli, *Jesus, Jonas, & Janus: The Leadership Triumvirate*, (Rochester, NY: Center for Professional Development Press, 2011), Part I, Chapter 9.

[6] Seals & Crofts, "We May Never Pass This Way Again," by James Seals and Darrell Crofts, In *Diamond Girl*, Warner Brothers, 1973, Album.

[7] Fr. George McInnis, *"Christ our God, Truth Incarnate" DVD*, Fathers of Mercy, 2010.

Appendices to Follow

Appendix A
Personal Budget

Budget Category		Budgeted	Spent	% of Take-Home	
Charity	(10%)				
Saving	(10%)				
Housing	(20%)				
Utilities	(5%)				
Food	(10%)				Take-Home Pay = $
Clothing	(5%)				Total Spent = $
Transportation	(10%)				Over or Under = $
Med./Health	(5%)				
Insurance	(10%)				
Personal	(5%)				
Recreation	(5%)				
Debts	(5%)				
Total	100%				

Appendix B
Life Insurance - Doe Family

Company	Phone Number	Policy Number	Type of Insurance	Amount of Insurance	Loan (If Any)	Coverage	Primary Beneficiary	Contingent Beneficiary
	Notes:							
	Notes:							
	Notes:							
	Notes:							
	Notes:							

Total Insurance on John Doe: $

203

Company	Phone Number	Policy Number	Type of Insurance	Amount of Insurance	Loan (If Any)	Coverage	Primary Beneficiary	Contingent Beneficiary
Notes:								
Notes:								
Total Insurance on Jane Doe: $								

Company	Phone Number	Policy Number	Type of Insurance	Amount of Insurance	Loan (If Any)	Coverage	Primary Beneficiary	Contingent Beneficiary
Notes:								
Notes:								
Total Insurance on Baby Doe: $								

Appendix C
Financial Records

	Location	Account or Certificate Number
Bank		
Stock		
Bond		
Safe Deposit Box		
Vehicle Title		
Real Estate		
Loan		

Appendix D

Inheritance Summary

Property to be Disbursed	Recipient	Is This in the Will?	Date to be Transferred

Appendix E
Family Tree

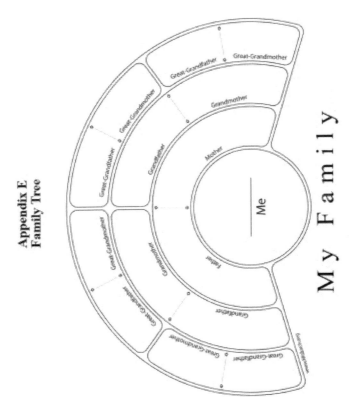

My Family

Me

Mother
Father
Grandmother
Grandfather
Great-Grandmother
Great-Grandfather
Great-Grandmother
Great-Grandfather
Great-Grandmother
Great-Grandfather
Great-Grandmother
Great-Grandfather

Appendix F
Legacy Plan

Type of Legacy	Goal	Action to be Taken
Family		
Professional		
Spirituality		

Appendix G
Lasting Impression Philosophy – Major Points

1. Lasting Impressions Awareness – Have you observed people influencing others by their behavior? What were your observations?

2. First Impressions – Can you remember a situation in which you recall someone left an impression on you? Is there an example in which your actions might have created an impression on others?

3. Speed of First Impressions – Are you conscious of situations in which you were quick in your assessment of others? Have you considered times that others may have quickly judged you?

4. Accuracy of First Impressions – Do you tend to be accurate in your perceptions of others? Have you formed an accurate perception of coworkers? Do you believe others have an accurate impression of you? Are some people more difficult to assess?

5. Longevity of First Impressions – Do you rely on impressions which were formed long ago? Have you reconsidered whether early perceptions are accurate?

6. Positive Impressions – Can you think of people who have had a positive influence on you? Have you ever thanked someone for their influence on you? Have you served as mentor to coworkers?

7. Negative Impressions – Do you recall people whose negative behavior created an impression on you? Have you considered that others' negative behavior can provide lessons worth learning as mistakes to avoid?

8. False Impressions – Are there times that you realized a first impression was not correct? How can we keep from being deceived by those who try to communicate a false impression?

9. Genuine Lasting Impressions – Are there people who have made genuine lasting impressions on you? What distinguishes genuine impressions from others? How do you guard against people who are artificial?

10. Lasting Impression As A Legacy – Can you identify people whose influence is so significant that you consider them a legacy? Are there reasons you may want to determine your own legacy?

11. Planning Your Legacy – Which goals are so important that they should be considered when determining your legacy? How will you pursue those goals in creating your legacy? How will coworkers remember you?

12. Lasting Impression Philosophy – If your lasting impression focus is successful, what will be your impact on others? What will your lasting influence look like? Does an awareness of lasting impressions change your behavior?

Bibliography

"9/11: The Twin Towers." *102 Minutes: The Untold Story of the Fight to Survive Inside the Twin Towers.* Narrated by Harry Pritchett and written by Jim Dwyer and Kevin Flynn. Discovery Channel, aired September 3, 2006, Television.

"2013 Harris Poll EquiTrend Rankings." Accessed July 19, 2013, http://www.harrisinteractive.com/Insights/EquiTrendRankings.aspx.

"A Tradition of Giving." Accessed August 23,2013,http://www.gatesfoundation. org/Who-We-Are/General-Information/History.

Aamodt, Michael G., and Custer, Heather. "Who Can Best Catch a Liar? A Meta-analysis of Individual Differences in Detecting Deception." *The Forensic Examiner* 15, no. 1 (2006): 6-11.

"About CNN Heroes", Accessed July 21, 2015, http://www.annenbergfoundation.org/node/50751.

Ahern, Tom. *Raising More Money With Your Newsletters Than You Ever Thought Possible.* Medfield, MA: Emerson & Church, 2005.

Albom, Mitch. *The Five People You Meet in Heaven.* New York: Hyperion, 2003.

Allers, Roger and Minkoff, Rob (Directors). *The Lion King. DVD.* 1994. Burbank, CA: Walt Disney Pictures, 2003.

Ambady, Nalini, and Rosenthal, Robert. "Half a Minute: Predicting Teacher Evaluations From Thin Slices of Nonverbal Behavior and Physical Attractiveness." *Journal of Personality and Social Psychology* 64, no. 3 (1993): 431-441.

Ambady, Nalini, and Rosenthal, Robert R. "Thin Slices of Expressive Behavior As Predictors of   Interpersonal Consequences: A Meta-Analysis." *Psychological Bulletin* 111, no. 2 (1992): 256.

Ambady, Nalini, Bernieri, Frank J., and Richeson, Jennifer A.. "Toward a Histology of Social Behavior: Judgmental Accuracy From Thin Slices of the Behavioral Stream." In *Advances in Experimental Social Psychology, edited by* Mark P. Zanna, 201-271. San Diego, CA: Academic Press, 2000.

Ambady, Nalini, Hallahan, Mark, and Rosenthal, Robert. "On Judging and Being Judged Accurately in Zero-Acquaintance Situations." *Journal of Personality and Social* Psychology 69 (1995): 518-529.

Ambady, Nalini, Krabbenhoft, Mary Anne, and Hogan, Daniel. "The 30-Sec Sale: Using Thin-   Slice Judgments to Evaluate Sales Effectiveness." *Journal of Consumer Psychology* 16, no. 1 (2006): 4-13.

Ambrose, Stephen E. *Undaunted Courage: Meriwether Lewis, Thomas Jefferson, and the Opening of the American West.* New York: Simon & Schuster, 1997.

Anderson, Eric D., Bella M. DePaulo, Bella M., Ansfield, Matthew E., Tickle, Jennifer J., and Green, Emily. "Beliefs About Cues to Deception: Mindless Stereotypes or Untapped Wisdom?" *Journal of Nonverbal Behavior* 23, no. 1 (1999): 67-89.

Antonakis, John, and Dalgas, Olaf. "Predicting Elections: Child's Play." *Science* 323, no. 5918 (2009): 1183.

Armstrong, Karen. *The Case for God.* New York: Random House, 2010.

Back, Mitja D., Stopfer, Juliane M., Vazire, Simine, Gaddis, Sam, Schmukle, Stefan C., Egloff, Boris, and Gosling, Samuel D. "Facebook Profiles Reflect Actual Personality, Not Self-Idealization." *Psychological Science* 21, no. 3 (2010): 372-374.

Bailey, Beth L. *America's Army.* Cambridge, MA: Harvard University Press, 2009.

Bar, Moshe, Neta, Marital, and Linz, Heather. "Very First Impressions." *Emotion* 6, no. 2 (2006): 269-278.

Barrick, Murray R., Patton, Gregory K., and Haugland, Shanna N. "Accuracy of Interviewer Judgments of Job Applicant Personality Traits." *Personnel Psychology* 53, no. 4 (2000): 925-951.

Bent, Samuel A. *Familiar Short Sayings of Great Men*. Boston: Ticknor and Company, 1887.

Biesanz, Jeremy, Human, Lauren J., Paquin, Annie-Claude, Chan, Meanne, Parisotto, Kate L., Sarracino Juliet, and Gillis, Randall L. "Do We Know When Our Impressions of Others Are Valid? Evidence for Realistic Accuracy Awareness in First Impressions of Personality." *Social Psychological and Personality Science* 2, no. 5 (2011): 452-459.

Blackman, Melinda C., and Funder, David C. "The Effect of Information on Consensus and Accuracy in Personality Judgment." *Journal of Experimental Social Psychology* 34 (1998): 164-181.

Blackman, Melinda. "What Yahoo CEO's False Bio Tells Us About Resume Fraud." Last modified May 12, 2012, http://www.cnn.com/2012/05/12/opinion/blackman-resume-fraud/index.html.

Bond, Charles F., and DePaulo, Bella M. "Accuracy of Deception Judgments." *Personality and Social Psychology Review* 10, no. 3 (2006): 214-234.

Boothman, Nicholas. *How to Make People Like You in 90 Seconds or Less*. New York: Workman, 2003.

Borkenau, Peter, and Liebler, Anette. "Trait Inferences: Sources Validity at Zero Acquaintance." *Journal of Personality & Social Psychology* 62 (1992): 645-657.

Bray, Chad, and Ef, Amir. "Madoff Pleads Guilty to Massive Fraud." The Wall Street Journal, March 11, 2013. http://www.theaustralian.com.au/business/ breaking-news/madoff-jailed-after-pleading-guilty/story-e6frg90f-1111119119325.

Brooks, Chad. "10 Minutes Is All Employers Need to Evaluate Job Candidates." Last modified September 19, 2012. http://www.cnbc.com/id/49087046/10_Minutes_Is_All_Employers_Need_to_Evaluate_Job_Candidates.

215

Burns, Dan. *The First 60 Seconds: Win the Job Interview Before It Begins.* Naperville, IL: Sourcebooks, Inc., 2009.

Buss, Dale. "McDonald's Brand Strength Keeps Its U.S. Customers Coming Back for More." Last modified January 21, 2013. http://www.brandchannel.com/home/post/2013/01/21/McDonalds-Satisfaction-Survey-012113.aspx.

Campion, Michael A., Palmer, David K., and Campion, James E. "A Review of Structure in the Selection Interview." *Personnel Psychology* 50 (1997): 655-702.

Carlston, Donal E., and Skowronski, John J. "Linking Versus Thinking: Evidence for the Different Associative and Attributional Bases of Spontaneous Trait Transference and Spontaneous Trait Inference." *Journal of Personality and Social Psychology* 89 (2005): 884-898.

Carney, Dana R., Colvin, C. Randall, and Hall, Judith A. "A Thin Slice Perspective on the Accuracy of First Impressions." *Journal of Research in Personality* 41, no. 5 (2007): 1054-1072.

Caroselli, Marlene. *Jesus, Jonas, & Janus: The Leadership Triumvirate.* Rochester, NY: Center for Professional Development Press, 2011.

Cervera, Leonor. "First Impressions Count." *USA Today*, Sept. 19, 1988: B1.

Cobb, Michael D., and Kuklinski, James H. "Changing Minds: Political Arguments and Political Persuasion." *American Journal of Political Science* 41, no. 1 (1997): 88-121.

Cohen, Arianne. "Make a Great First Impression." *Health* 21, no.4 (2007): 159-160.

"Consumer Edge Insight's Restaurant Demand Tracker." Accessed July 27, 2013, http://consumeredgeinsight.com/ trackers/industry/restaurants.

Covey, Stephen. *First Things First.* New York: Free Press, 1994.

Crawford, Matthew T., McCarthy, Randy J., Kjaerstad, Hanne L., and Skowronski, John J. "Inferences Are For Doing: The Impact of Approach and Avoidance States on the Generation of Spontaneous Trait Inferences." *Personality and Social Psychology Bulletin* 39, no. 3, (2013): 267-278.

Cronkite, IV, Walter, and Isserman, Maurice. *Cronkite's War: His World War II Letters Home.* Washington, DC: National Geographic Society, 2013.

"Dannon Agrees to Drop Exaggerated Health Claims for Activia Yogurt and DanActive Dairy Drink." Last modified December 15, 2010, http://www.ftc.gov/opa/2010/12/dannon.shtm.

Darley, John M., & Fazio, Russell H. "Expectancy Confirmation Processes Arising in the Social Interaction Sequence." *American Psychologist* 35, no.10 (1980): 867-881.

Demarais, Ann, and White, Valerie. *What You Don't Know About How Others See You.* New York: Bantam Dell, Random House, 2004.

Denby, David. "Last Impressions," *New Yorker* 82, no. 11 (2006): 95-97.

DeSario, Jack, and Mason, William D. *Dr. Sam Sheppard on Trial: The Prosecutors and the Marilyn Sheppard Murder.* Kent, OH: Kent State University Press, 2003.

DeWitt, Katharine, Assistant Editor. "Nursing News and Announcements." *The American Journal of Nursing* 18, no. 2 (1917): 167.

DiGregorio, Sarah, "The Miracle in My Mother's Pudding," *Parade Magazine* (May 11, 2014): 8.

"Down the Sink: Coke." Accessed July 3, 2013, http://www.time.com/time/specials/packages/article/0,28804,1913612_1913610_1913608,00.html.

Dromgoole, Will Allen. "The Bridge Builder." In *Father: An Anthology of Verse, edited by* Margery Doud and Cleo M. Parsley, *86. New York:* E.P. Dutton & Company, 1931.

Dunn, Troy. (Narrator), "*APB with Troy Dunn – The Gift/Forgiven*", TNT, aired Jan. 17, 2014, Television.

Dwyer, Jim, and Flynn, Kevin. *102 Minutes: The Unforgettable Story of the Fight to Survive Inside the Twin Towers.* New York, NY: Times Books, Henry Holt and Company, 2005.

Einstein, Albert. *The World As I See It* (translated by Alan Harris). London: J. Lane, 1935.

Eisenberg, John. *That First Season.* New York: Houghton Mifflin Harcourt Publishing, 2009.

Ekman, Paul. *Emotions Revealed: Recognizing Faces and Feelings to Improve Communication   and Emotional Life.* New York: Owl Books, Henry Holt and Company, LLC., 2003.

Emerson, Ralph Waldo. "American Civilization." *The Atlantic Monthly* 9 (1862): 506.

Enright, Dominique. *The Wicked Wit of Winston Churchill.* London: Michael O'Mara Books Limited, 2001.

Evenson, Renee. "Making a Great First Impression." *Techniques: Connecting Education & Careers* 82, no. 5 (2007): 14.

Fahim, Kareem, Staba, David, and Delaqueriere, Alain. "The Suspect in 3 Murders and 8 Rapes Blended In." *New York Times*, Jan. 18, 2007, B1.

Family of Vince Lombardi. "Famous Quotes by Vince Lombardi." Accessed April 14, 2013, http://www.vincelombardi.com/quotes.html.

Fee, Susan. "Make a Positive First Impression." *Training & Development* 59, no. 4 (2005), 14.

Fiske, Susan T., Lin, Monica, and Neuberg, Steven L. "The Continuum Model: Ten Years Later." In *Dual-Process Models in Social Psychology*, edited by Shelly Chaiken and Yaacov Trope, 231-254. New York: The Guilford Press, 2009.

218

Flora, Carlin. "The Once-Over: Can You Trust First Impressions?" *Psychology Today* 37, no. 3 (2004): 60.

Ford, Henry. *Ford News*, (1922): p. 2.

"Fortune 100 Best Companies to Work For: Google." Accessed August 23, 2013, http://money.cnn.com/magazines/fortune/best-companies/2013/snapshots/1.html.

"Free Family Tree PDF Charts." Accessed April 14, 2013, http://www.misbach.org/freecharts/ kids-chart.html.

Frick, Robert. "Why We Fall for Scams." *Kiplinger's Personal Finance* 65, no. 5 (2011): p. 24.

Friends of the Beartooth All-American Road,."On the Wild Side of Yellowstone." Accessed March 16, 2013, http://www.beartoothhighway.com/wildRoad/index.html.

Funder, David C. "Accurate Personality Judgment." *Current Directions in Psychological Science* 21, no. 3 (2012): 177-182.

Funder, David C. and Colvin, C. Randall. "Friends and Strangers: Acquaintanceship, Agreement, and the Accuracy of Personality Judgment." *Journal of Personality and Social Psychology* 55, no. 1 (1988): 149-158.

Funder, David C. "Errors and Mistakes: Evaluating the Accuracy of Social Judgment." *Psychological Bulletin*, 101 (1987): 75-90.

Gallagher, Patrick, Fleeson, William, and Hoyle, Rick H. "A Self-Regulatory Mechanism for Personality Trait Stability: Contra-Trait Effort." *Social Psychological & Personality Science* 2, no. 4 (2011): 335-342.

Gates, Bill, and Gates, Melinda. "Letter From Bill and Melinda Gates." Accessed August 23, 2013, http://www.gatesfoundation.org/Who-We-Are/General-Information/Letter-from-Bill-and-Melinda-Gates.

Gladwell, Malcolm. *Blink: The Power of Thinking Without Thinking* New York: Little, Brown, and Company, 2005.

Goffman, Erving. *The Presentation of Self in Everyday Life.* New York: Doubleday, 1959.

"Google Giving." Accessed August 23, 2013, http://www.google.com/giving/.

Graham, Billy. *Hope for the Troubled Heart: Finding God in the Midst of Pain.* New York: Bantam Books, 1993.

Grasz, Jennifer. "Nearly Three-in-Ten Employers Have Caught a Fake Reference on a Job Application. " Last modified November 28, 2012, http://www.careerbuilder.com/share/aboutus/pressreleasesdetail.aspx?s d=11%2f28%2f2012&sc_cmp1=cb_pr727_&siteid=cbpr&id=p r727&ed=12%2f31%2f2012.

Gray, Heather M. "To What Extent, and Under What Conditions, are First Impressions Valid?" In *First Impressions*, edited by. Nalini Ambady and John J. Skowronski, 121. New York: The Guilford Press, 2008.

Greene, Lorne. "Mirror of a Man." *Bonanza.* Directed by Lewis Allen and written by A.I. Bezzerides. NBC, aired March 31, 1963. Television.

Gregg, Aiden P., Seibt, Beate, and Banaji, Mahzarin R. "Easier Done Than Undone: Asymmetry in the Malleability of Implicit Preferences." *Journal of Personality and Social Psychology* 90, no. 1 (2006): 13.

Grill-Spector, Kalanit, and Kanwisher, Nancy. "Visual Recognition: As Soon As
You Know It Is There, You Know What It Is." *Psychological Science* 16, no. 2 (2005): 152-160.

Grill-Spector, Kalanit, Knouf, Nicholas, and Kanwisher, Nancy. "The Fusiform Face Area Sub Serves Face Perception, Not Generic Within-Category Identification." *Nature Neuroscience* 7 (2004): 555-562.

Grimm, Jacob L., and Grimm, Wilhelm C. *Children's and Household Tales.* Kassel, Germany: Grimm Brothers, 1812.

Guardiola, Fr. Louis. *The Catechetical Tour of The Divine Mercy Chapel of The Fathers of Mercy of The Immaculate Conception of the Blessed Virgin Mary of South Union, Kentucky.* Auburn, KY: The Fathers of Mercy, 2013.

Hall, A.W. *Great Thoughts From Master Minds.* London: Smith Publishing Company, Vol. V, 1908.

Hamilton, David R. *Why Kindness Is Good for You.* Carlsbad, CA: Hay House, Inc., 2010.

"Happy 85th Birthday Gerber!" Accessed August 24, 2013, http://news.gerber.com/news/happy-85th-birthday-gerber-let-245121.

Harben, Katherine. "Where the Heart Finds a Home." The Ohio State University Alumni Association. Last modified Jan. 21, 2010, http://www.ohiostatealumni.org/media/Pages/WheretheHeartFindsaHome.aspx.

Harris, Monica J. and Garris, Christopher P. "You Never Get a Second Chance to Make a First Impression: Behavioral Consequences of First Impressions." In *First Impressions*, edited by Nalini Ambady and John J. Skowronski, 148. New York: The Guilford Press, 2008.

Harris Interactive. "The Harris Poll Reputation Quotient." Accessed July 9, 2013, http://www.harrisinteractive.com/vault/2013%20RQ%20Summary%20Report%20FINAL.pdf.

Haselton, Martie G., and Funder, David C. "The Evolution of Accuracy and Bias in Social Judgment." In *Evolution and Social Psychology,* edited by Mark Schaller, Jeffry A. Simpson, and Douglas T. Kenrick, 15-37. New York: Psychology Press, 2006.

"Heritage." Accessed August 24, 2013, http://www.gerber.com/AllStages/About/Heritage.aspx.

Hogarth, Robin M. *Educating Intuition.* Chicago: University of Chicago Press, 2001.

"How It All Started", July 21,2015, http://www.americasgrowarow.org/about/.

Human, Lauren J., Biesanz, Jeremy C., Parisotto, Kate L., and Dunn, Elizabeth W. "Your Best Self Helps Reveal Your True Self: Positive Self-Presentation Leads to More Accurate Personality Impressions." *Social Psychological and Personality Science* 3, no. 1 (2012): 23-30.

Hutchins, David. *Quality Circles Handbook.* New York, NY: Nichols Publishing Company, 1985.

Isaacowitz, Derek M., Lockenhoff, Corinna E., Lane, Richard D., Wright, Ron, Sechrest, Lee, Riedel, Robert, and Costa, Paul T. "Age Differences in Recognition of Emotion in Lexical Stimuli and Facial Expressions." *Psychology and Aging* 22 (2007): 147-159.

Ispas, Alexa. "Creating Legacy Manifesto." Last modified June 9, 2010, http://www.alexaispas.com/creating-legacy-manifesto.

Ispas, Alexa. "This Question Can Save Your Life." Last modified June 16, 2010, http://www.alexaispas.com.

Jamal, Nina, and Lindenberger, Judith. "How to Make a Great First Impression." *Business Knowhow*, Accessed December 29, 2011, http://www.businessknowhow.com/growth/dress-impression.htm.

Jayson, Sharon. "Are Voters Taking Candidates at Face Value?" *USA Today*, Oct. 23, 2007:4D.

Jeremiah, David. "The Futility of Life." *Turning Point.* American Family Radio. Delphos, OH: WBIE, February 3, 2013, Radio.

Jolij, Jacob. "One-Tenth of a Second to Make a First Impression: Early Visual Evoked Potentials Correlate With Perceived Trustworthiness of Faces." *International Journal of Psychophysiology* 77, no. 3 (2010): 207.

Joyce, Eric. "Remembering the Final Days of America's 50-Star Flag Designer Bob Heft." Last modified December 14, 2009, http://www.mlive.com/news/saginaw/index.ssf/2009/12/remembering_the_final_days_of.html.

Kahneman, Daniel, and Tversky, Amos. "Causal Schemas in Judgments Under Uncertainty." In *Judgment Under Uncertainty: Heuristics and Biases,* edited by Daniel Kahneman and Amos Tversky, 117. Cambridge, UK: Cambridge University Press, 1982.

Kardes, Frank R. "When Should Consumers and Managers Trust Their Intuition?" *Journal of Consumer Psychology* 16, no. 1 (2006): 21.

Kenny, David A., Horner, Caryl, Kashy, Deborah A., and Chu, Ling-chuan. "Consensus at Zero Acquaintance: Replication, Behavioral Cues, and Stability." *Journal of Personality and Social Psychology* 62, (1992):88-97.

Kenny, David A., and West, Tessa V. "Zero Acquaintance: Definitions, Statistical Model, Findings, and Processes." In *First Impressions,* edited by Nalini Ambady and John J. Skowronski, 138. New York: The Guilford Press, 2008.

Krieger, Richard Alan. *Civilization's Quotations: Life's Ideal.* New York: Algora Publishing, 2002.

Krendl, Anne C., Magoon, Nicole S., Hull, Jay G., and Heatherton, Todd F. "Judging a Book By Its Cover: The Differential Impact of Attractiveness on Predicting One's Acceptance to High- or Low-Status Social Groups." *Journal of Applied Social Psychology* 41, no. 10 (2011): 2548.

Kreyche, Gerald F. "How to Make a 'Last'-ing Impression." *USA Today Magazine* 129, no. 2658 (2000): 82.

Lakin, Jessica L. "Automatic Cognitive Processes and Nonverbal Communication." In *The Sage Handbook of Nonverbal Communication,* edited by Valerie L. Manusov and Miles L. Patterson, 59-77. Thousand Oaks, CA: Sage, 2006.

Lavington, Camille. *You've Only Got Three Seconds: How to Make the Right Impression in Your Business and Social Life.* New York: Doubleday, 1998.

"Lawn Tractors." *Consumer Reports Buying Guide* 77, no. 13 (2013): 79-81.

Levashina, Julia, and Campion, Michael A. "A Model of Faking Likelihood in the Employment Interview." *International Journal of Selection and Assessment* 14, no. 4 (2006): 300.

Levering, Robert, and Moskowitz, Milton. "100 Best Companies to Work For: How We Pick the 100 Best." August 23, 2013, http://money.cnn.com/magazines/fortune/best-companies/2013/faq/index.html?iid=bc.

Levesque, Maurice J. and Kenny, David A. "Accuracy of Behavioral Predictions at Zero Acquaintance: A Social Relations Analysis." *Journal of Personality & Social Psychology*, 65, no. 6 (1993): 1178-1189.

Lewis, C.S. *Mere Christianity.* New York: The MacMillan Company, 1952.

Lewis, Lionel S. "How Madoff Did It: Victims' Accounts." *Society* 48, no. 1 (2011): 75.

Lievens, Filip, and Peeters, Helga. "Interviewers' Sensitivity to Impression\ Management Tactics in Structured Interviews." *European Journal of Psychological Assessment* 24, no. 3 (2008): 179.

"LifeLock Will Pay $12 Million to Settle Charges by the FTC and 35 States That Identity Theft Prevention and Data Security Claims Were False." modified March 9, 2010,http://www.ftc.gov/opa/2010/03/lifelock.shtm.

"LifeLock to Pay $100 Million to Consumers to Settle FTC Charges it Violated 2010 Order." Last modified December 17, 2015, https://www.ftc.gov/news-events/press-releases/2015/12/lifelock-pay-100-million-consumers-settle-ftc-charges-it-violated.

Little, Anthony C., Burriss, Robert P., Jones, Benedict C., and Roberts, S. Craig. "Facial Appearance Affects Voting Decisions." *Evolution and Human Behavior* 28, no. 1(2007): 18-27.

Lorenz, Kate. "How to Conquer the First Impression." Last modified September 24, 2007, http://www.careerbuilder.com/Article/CB-409-Getting-Hired-How-to-Conquer-the-First-Impression/.

Maclaren, Alexander. *A Year's Ministry, Volume 2*. London: Office of the Christian Commonwealth, 1884.

Mann, Samantha, Vrij, Albert, Leal, Sharon, Granhag, Par A., Warmelink, Lara, and Forrester, Dave. "Windows to the Soul? Deliberate Eye Contact as a Cue to Deceit." *Journal of Nonverbal Behavior* 36 (2012): 205-215.

Marriott, J. Willard, and Brown, Kathi A. *The Spirit to Serve: Marriott's Way*. New York, NY: Harper Collins, 1997.

Martin, Douglas. "Walter Cronkite, 92, Dies; Trusted Voice of TV News." Last modified July 17, 2009, http://www.nytimes.com/2009/07/18/us/18cronkite.html?pagewanted=all.

Mast, Marianne S., Bangerter, Adrian, Bulliard, Celine, and Aerni, Gaelle. "How Accurate Are Recruiters' First Impressions of Applicants in Employment Interviews?" *International Journal of Selection and Assessment* 19, no. 2 (2011): 206.

Mattes, Kyle, Spezio, Michael, Hackjin, Kim, Todorov, Alexander, Adolphs, Ralph, and Alvarez, R. Michael. "Predicting Election Outcomes from Positive and Negative Trait Assessments of Candidate Images." *Political Psychology* 31, no. 1 (2010): 41-58.

McCarthy, Liz. (Senior Vice President and Head of Corporate Communications). *"Parallels."* New York Life Insurance Company, aired Dec. 22, 2012, Television commercial.

McCarthy, Randy J., and Skowronski, John J. "The Interplay of Controlled and Automatic Processing in the Expression of Spontaneously Inferred Traits: A PDP Analysis." *Journal of Personality and Social Psychology* 100, no. 2 (2011): 229-240.

McCarthy, Randy J., and Skowronski, John J. "What Will Phil Do Next? Spontaneously Inferred Traits Influence Predictions of Behavior." *Journal of Experimental Social Psychology* 47, (2011): 321-332.

McInnis, Fr. George. *Christ Our God, Truth Incarnate.* DVD. Fathers of Mercy, 2010.

McConnell, Allen R., Rydell, Robert J., Strain, Laura M., and Mackie, Dianne M. "Forming Implicit and Explicit Attitudes Toward Individuals: Social Group Association Cues." *Journal of Personality & Social Psychology* 94 (2008): 792-807.

McMullen, Troy. "Dannon to Pay $45M to Settle Yogurt Lawsuit." Last modified February 26, 2010, http://abcnews.go.com/Business/dannon-settles-lawsuit/story?id=9950269.

Mee, Cheryl L. "First Impressions Last." *Nursing* 36, no. 6 (2006): 6.

Mee, Cheryl L. "Painting a Portrait: How You Can Shape Nursing's Image." *Imprint* 53, no. 5 (2006): 47.

Mehrabian,Albert. *Silent Messages: Implicit Communication of Emotions and Attitudes.* Belmont, CA: Wadsworth Publishing, 1981.

Merriam-Webster. "Merriam-Webster.com.*"* Accessed Dec. 27, 2012, http://www.merriam-webster.com/dictionary/legacy.

Michaud, Chris. "Madoff Says He Is Happier in Prison Than Free." The New York Times, Last modified Oct. 27, 2011, http://www.reuters.com/article/2011/10/27/us-madoff-interview-idUSTRE79Q56H20111027.

"Milton the Man." Accessed July 3, 2013, http://www.miltonhershey.com/milton_knowledge.html.

Michener, H. Andrew, DeLamater, John D., and Myers, Daniel J. *Social Psychology.* Belmont, CA: Wadsworth, 2003.

Mitchell, Joni. *Big Yellow Taxi.* © 1970 by Reprise. RS 20906. Single.

Mitchell, Mary. *The First Five Minutes: How to Make a Great First Impression in Any Business Situation.* New York: John Wiley & Sons, Inc., 1998.

"More Than Half of Companies in the Top Ten World Economies Have Been Affected By a Bad Hire, According to CareerBuilder Survey." Last modified May 8, 2013, http://www.careerbuilder.com/share/aboutus/pressreleasesdetail.aspx?sd=5%2F8%2F2013&id=pr757&ed=12%2F31%2F2013.

Muir, Hazel. "Their Brains Lit Up Across a Crowded Room." *New Scientist* 172,
   no. 2312 (2001): 6.

Naumann, Laura P., Vazire, Simine, Rentfrow, Peter, and Gosling, Samuel D. "Personality Judgments Based on Physical Appearance." *Personality and Social Psychology Bulletin* 35, no. 12 (2009): 1661.

Nike, Inc. *Nike Statement on Lance Armstrong.* Accessed Oct. 17, 2012, http://www.nikeinc.com/news/nike-statement-on-lance-armstrong.

Olivola, Christina, and Todorov, Alexander. "Elected in 100 Milliseconds: Appearance-Based Trait Inferences and Voting." *Journal of Nonverbal Behavior* 34 (2010): 83-110.

Olivola, Christopher, and Todorov, Alexander. "Fooled by First Impressions? Reexamining the Diagnostic Value of Appearance-Based Inferences." *Journal of Experiential Social Psychology* 46 (2010): 315-324.

Osler, Sir William. *Aequanimitas.* Philadelphia: P. Blakiston's Sons & Company, 1904.

"Our Legacy; Our Story – The Walton Family Foundation." Accessed September 6, 2013, http://www.waltonfamilyfoundation.org/about.

"P & G Corporate Newsroom." Accessed August 24, 2013, http://news.pg.com/external_recognition.

Palmer, Stephanie. "Put Your Best Face Forward." *Shape* 27, no. 7 (2008): 37.

Peeters, Helga, and Lievens, Filip. "Verbal and Nonverbal Impression Management Tactics in Behavior Description and Situational Interviews." *International Journal of Selection and Assessment* 14, no. 3 (2006): 206-222.

Pelham, Dennis. "Driver Gets Prison for Crash That Killed Community Leader."
Daily Telegram, December 15, 2012, 1.

Pham, Vu H., and Miyake, Lisa. *Impressive First Impressions: A Guide to the Most Important 30 Seconds (and 30 Years) of Your Career.* Santa Barbara, CA: Praeger, 2010.

Phillips, Stone. (Anchor), *Dateline NBC.* Produced by David Corvo. NBC, aired May 17, 1995. Television.

Plato. *The Apology of Socrates.* Translated by D.F. Nevill. London: F.E. Robinson & Company, 1901.

Pollard, C. William. *The Soul of the Firm.* Grand Rapids, MI: Zondervan Publishing House, 1996.

Porter, Stephen, and ten Brinke, Leanne. " Dangerous Decisions: A Theoretical Framework for Understanding How Judges Assess Credibility in the Courtroom." *Law and Human Behavior* 14 (2009): 119-134.

Porter, Stephen, England, Laura, Juodis, Marcus, ten Brinke, Leanne, and Wilson, Kevin. "Is the Face a Window to the Soul? Investigation of the Validity of Intuitive Judgments of the Trustworthiness of Human Faces." *Canadian Journal of Behavioral Science* 40, no. 3 (2008): 171-177.

Porter, Stephen, ten Brinke, Leanne, and Gustaw, Chantal,."Dangerous Decisions: The Impact of First Impressions of Trustworthiness On the Evaluation of Legal Evidence and Defendant Culpability." *Psychology, Crime & Law* 16, no. 6 (2010): 479.

Posthuma, Richard A., Morgeson, Frederick P., and Campion, Michael A.. "Beyond Employment Interview Validity: A Comprehensive Narrative Review of Recent Research and Trends Over Time." *Personnel Psychology* 55 (2002): 1-81.

Powell, Chris. "GMA: Episode 62 Kate Middleton, Prince William Baby Girl Rumors." *Good Morning America.* American Broadcasting Company, aired March 6, 2013, Television.

Ramsey, Dave. "Budgeting Tools: Dave's Budgeting Forms." Accessed October 2, 2013, http://a248.e.akamai.net/f/1611/26335/9h/dramsey.download. akamai.com/23572/daveramsey.com/media/pdf/forms/fpu_monthly_ cash_flow_plan_forms.pdf.

Ramsey, Dave. *The Total Money Makeover.* Nashville, TN: Thomas Nelson, Inc., 2003.

Rasmussen, Frederick N. "A Half-Century Ago, New 50-Star American Flag Debuted in Baltimore." Last modified July 2, 2010, http://articles.baltimoresun.com/2010-07-02/news/bs-md-backstory- 1960-flag-20100702_1_48-star-flag-blue-canton-fort-mchenry.

Regan, Dennis T., Straus, Ellen, and Fazio, Russell H. "Liking and the Attribution Process." *Journal of Experimental Social Psychology* 10 (1974): 385-397.

Rentfrow, Peter J., and Gosling, Samuel D. "Message in a Ballad: The Role of Music Preferences in Interpersonal Perception." *Psychological Science* 17 (2006): 236-242.

"Report of Examination." *Federal Bureau of Investigation* (1998): (29D-O1C-LR-35063).

"Residential." Accessed August 21, 2013, http://www.deere.com/wps/dcom/ enUS/industry/residential/residential.page?

Robinson, J.J. "Security in the Spotlight." Last modified January 23, 2009, http://www.information-age.com/channels/security-and-continuity/ perspectives-and-trends/990012/security-in-the-spotlight.html.

Rohn, Jim. "The Importance of Leaving a Legacy." Accessed April 14, 2013, http://www.jimrohn.com/index.php?main_page=page&id=1294.

Ross, Lee, Lepper, Mark R., and Hubbard, Michael. "Perseverance in Self-Perception and Social Perception: Biased Attributional Processes in the Debriefing Paradigm." *Journal of Personality and Social Psychology* 32, no. 5 (1975): 880.

Rule, Ann. The Stranger Beside Me. New York: Pocket Books, 2009.

Rule, Nicholas O., and Ambady, Nalini. "First Impressions: Peeking at the Neural Underpinnings." In *First Impressions,* edited by Nalini Ambady and John J. Skowronski, 42. New York: The Guilford Press, 2008.

Rule, Nicholas O., and Ambady, Nalini. "The Face of Success." *Psychological Science* 19, no. 2 (2008): 109-111.

Rydell, Robert J., McConnell, Allen R., Mackie, Diane M., and Strain, Laura M. "Of Two Minds: Forming and Changing Valence Inconsistent Implicit and Explicit Attitudes." *Psychological Science* 17, no. 11 (2006): 954-958.

Rymer, Zachary D. "Why Mark McGwire Doesn't Deserve to Be In Cooperstown. " Bleacher   Report, Last modified December 6, 2012, http://bleacherreport.com/articles/1434532-hall-of-fame-vote-2013-why-mark-mcgwire-doesnt-deserve-to-be-in-cooperstown.

Salgado, Jesus F., and Moscoso, Silvia. "Comprehensive Meta-analysis of the Construct Validity of the Employment Interview." *European Journal of Work Organizational Psychology* 11 (2002): 299-324.

Schaller, Mark. "Evolutionary Bases of First Impressions." In *First Impressions,* edited by Nalini Ambady and John J. Skowronski, 15-34. New York: The Guilford Press, 2008.

Schwartz, Stephen, Chenowith, Kristin, and Menzel, Idina, "Wicked: A New Musical", CD, Decca Broadway, 2003.

Schweitzer, Albert. *"Thoughts for Our Times,"* edited by Erica Anderson, 51. Mount Vernon, NY: Peter Pauper Press, 1975.

Seals & Crofts, "We May Never Pass This Way Again," by James Seals and Darrell Crofts, In *Diamond Girl*, Warner Brothers, 1973, Album.

Sinek, Simon. *Leaders Eat Last: Why Some Teams Pull Together and Others Don't.* New York, NY: Portfolio/Penguin, 2014.

Skowronski, John J., and Carlston, Donal E. "Negativity and Extremity Biases in Impression Formation: A Review of Explanations." *Psychological Bulletin 105, no. 1 (1989):* 131.

Slovic, Paul. "Perceived Risk, Trust, and Democracy." *Risk Analysis* 13 (1993): 675-682.

Smith, Jacquelyn. "America's Most Reputable Companies." April 24, 2013, http://www.forbes.com/sites/jacquelynsmith/2013/04/24/americas-most-reputable-companies-2/?utm_source=huffingtonpost.com&utm_medium=partner&utm_campaign=most+reputable+companies&partner=huffpo.

Spink, Kathryn. *Mother Teresa: An Authorized Biography.* New York: Harper Collins, 2011.

Strobel, Lee. *The Case for Faith.* Grand Rapids, MI: Zondervan, 2000.

Sunnafrank, Michael, and Ramirez, Artemio. "At First Sight: Persistent Relational Effects of Get-Acquainted Conversations." *Journal of Social and Psychological Relationships* 21, no. 3 (2004): 361-379.

Taylor, Paul J., and Small, Bruce. "Asking Applicants What They Would Do Versus What They Did Do: A Meta-analytic Comparison of Situational and Past Behaviour Employment Interview Questions." *Journal of Occupational and Organizational Psychology* 75 (2002): 277-294.

"The Gerber Foundation." Accessed August 24, 2013, http://www.gerberfoundation.org/home/history.

"Thieves Trick Salvation Army Bell ringer, Steal Kettle," Modified December 4, 2014, WSOCTV Charlotte, NC, http://www.wsoctv.com/news/ news/local/thieves-trick-salvation-army-bell-ringer-steal-ket/njLs9/.

"The Power of Purpose." Accessed August 24, 2013, http://www.pg.com/en_US/company/purpose_people/index.shtml.

"The Walton Family Foundation." Accessed September 6, 2013, http://www.waltonfamilyfoundation.org/grantees.

Todorov, Alexander, Baron, Sean G, and Oosterhof, Nickolaas N. "Evaluating Face Trustworthiness: A Model Based Approach." *Social Cognitive and Affective Neuroscience* 3, no. 2 (2008): 126.

Todorov, Alexander, Mandisodza, Anesu N., Goren, Amir, and Hall, Crystal C. "Inferences of Competence from Faces Predict Election Outcomes." *Science* 308 (2005): 1623-1626.

Todorov, Alexander, Pakrashi, Manish, and Oosterhof, Nickolaas N. "Evaluating Faces on Trustworthiness After Minimal Time Exposure." *Social Cognition* 27, no. 6 (2009): 813.

Turner, Nick, and Bass, Dina. "Yahoo Investor Steps Up Pressure to Have CEO Fired." Last modified May 5, 2012, http://www.businessweek.com/news/2012-05-05/yahoo-board-to-review-ceo-credentials-after-criticism#p1.

United States Conference of Catholic Bishops. *The New American Bible.* Washington: United States Conference of Catholic Bishops, 2002.

Vasco, Rev. Msgr. Christopher P. *The Twenty-Third Psalm: A Reflection on the Passion of Jesus Christ.* Swanton, OH: Author, 2013.

Vrij, Albert. *Detecting Lies and Deceit: Pitfalls and Opportunities.* Chichester, UK: Wiley, 2008.

von Hildebrand, Dietrich. *Liturgy and Personality: The Healing Power of Formal Prayer.* Manchester, NH: Sophia Institute Press, 1960.

von Schiller, Johann Christoph Friedrich. *Wallenstein's Lager.* Translated by M. Verkruzen. Hamburg: The Author, 1899.

Walker-Andrews, Arlene S. "Infants' Perception of Expressive Behaviors: Differentiation of Multimodal Information." *Psychological Bulletin* 121 (1997): 437-456.

Walton, Sam, and Huey, John. *Sam Walton: Made in America.* New York, NY: Doubleday, 1992.

Walton-Moss, Benita J., Manganello, Jennifer, Frye, Victoria, and Campbell, Jacquelyn C. "Risk Factors for Intimate Partner Violence and Associated Injury Among Urban Women." *Journal of Community Health 30*, no. 5 (2005): 377–389.

Washington, Booker T. *Up From Slavery: An Autobiography.* New York: Doubleday, Page & Company, 1907.

Washington, H.A., editor. *The Writings of Thomas Jefferson: Being His Autobiography, Correspondence, Reports, Messages, Addresses, and Other Writings, Official and Private.* Washington, DC: Taylor & Maury, 1854.

Willis, Janine, and Todorov, Alexander. "First Impressions: Making Up Your Mind After a 100-Ms Exposure to a Face." *Psychological Science* 17, no.7 (2006): 597.

Winerman, Lea. "'Thin Slices' of Life." *Monitor on Psychology* 36, no. 3 (2005): 54.

Winfrey, Oprah. "Oprah and Lance Armstrong: The Worldwide Exclusive, Part 1." *Oprah's Next Chapter.* Oprah Winfrey Network, aired Jan. 17, 2013, Television.

Winston, Joel S., Strange, Bryan A., O'Doherty, John, and Dolan, Raymond J. "Automatic and Intentional Brain Responses During Evaluation of Trustworthiness of Faces." *Nature Neuroscience* 5, no. 3 (2002): 277-283.

Wyatt, Edward. "LifeLock Settles With F.T.C. Over Charges of Deception."
Last modified March 9, 2010,
http://www.nytimes.com/2010/03/10/business/10ftc.html.

Wyer, Natalie A. "You Never Get a Second Chance to Make a First (Implicit)
Impression: The Role of Elaboration in the Formation and Revision of
Implicit Impressions." *Social Cognition* 28, no. 1 (2010):1-19.

Zaslow, Jeffrey. "First Impressions Get Faster." *The Wall Street Journal* 247,
no. 39 (2006): D4.

Zenger, Jack and Folkman, Joseph, "The Trickle-Down Effect of Good (and
Bad) Leadership", Harvard Business Review, last modified Jan. 14,
2016, https://hbr.org/2016/01/the-trickle-down-effect-of-good-and-bad-
leadership.

"Determining Your Legacy" was written to illuminate the impact of impressions on our lives and to enhance our ability to perceive those influences. The power of impressions is revealed through real-life stories, and the significance of lasting impressions on life's decisions is clarified. Once we realize the power of genuine impressions, we may determine our lasting legacy for others as a contribution to those who follow us.

Dr. Larry Zachrich is a lifelong educator. He has taught high school teenagers, college students, and factory workers. Over a 39-year career at Northwest State Community College, Dr. Zachrich has served as a business professor, Dean of Business, Dean of Engineering Technologies, and Dean of Arts & Sciences. He spent time in the manufacturing sector and has assisted Fortune 500 companies as a consultant.

Reflecting on an educational profession which values career preparation and learned skills, Dr. Zachrich began to witness the power of impressions that people communicate to each other. The teacher became a student of human behavior, as he realized the opportunity to learn from impressions communicated continuously by others and the valuable legacies they provide. "Determining Your Legacy" summarizes the power of impressions and the opportunity for each of us to develop a lasting legacy which benefits others.

Future books clarifying the power of impressions will follow from Power of Impressions Publishing.

Larry Zachrich

www.larryzachrich.com

235